Carving 18th Century American Furniture Elements

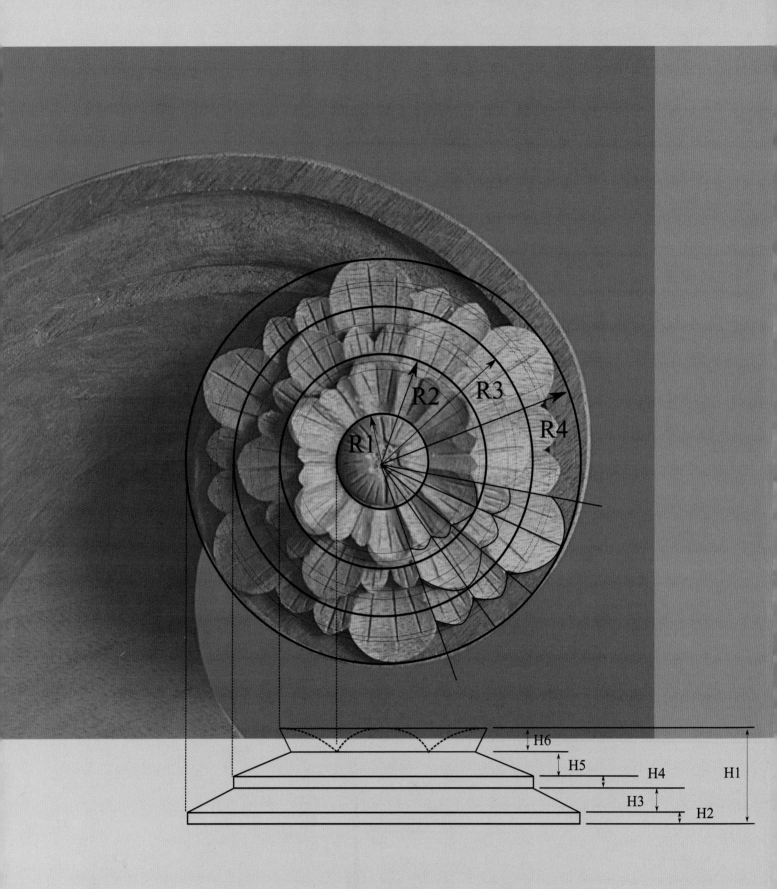

Carving 18th Century American Furniture Elements

10 Step-by-Step Projects for Furniture Makers

by Tony Kubalak

Linden Publishing
Fresno

Editor: Richard Sorsky
Cover design: James Goold
Photography: Tony Kubalak and Barb Slagg
Design and layout: Maura J. Zimmer

ISBN 13: 978-1-933502-32-8

Printed in China

35798642

Woodworking is inherently dangerous. Your safety is your responsibility.
Neither Linden Publishing nor the author assume any responsibility for any injuries or accidents.

Library of Congress Cataloging-in-Publication Data

Kubalak, Tony.
Carving 18th century American furniture elements : 10 step-by-step projects for furniture makers/by Tony Kubalak.
    p. cm.
ISBN 978-1-933502-32-8 (pbk. : alk. paper)
1. Furniture making--Amateurs' manuals. 2. Furniture--United States--History--18th century. 3. Furniture--
Reproduction--Amateurs' manuals. 4. Furniture making. I. Title.
TT195.K92 2010
684.1--dc22
        2010018787

To my wife Barb and my son Peter who really do make everything worthwhile.

Acknowledgements

Joel Ficke for material review, suggestions and comments.

Gene Landon for inspiration and motivation.

Irion Furniture Company for letting me study some of their work.

Table of Contents

Foreword

Over the many years that I have been teaching the construction of Eighteenth Century American furniture, I have had the privilege and opportunity to meet and instruct many serious and talented people. Tony Kubalak is one such student. For years Tony traveled 2,200 miles to attend my weekend classes at Olde Mill Cabinet Shoppe in York, Pennsylvania. He did this multiple times per year for many years.

Tony's passion for learning technique and correctness of line and scale were noteworthy. He would labor over a new motif until it was perfect. His passion for the correct look is evident in his execution of a finished furniture form.

With these fond memories of Tony as my student, I look forward to the success of his book on carving.

—Eugene E. Landon

Introduction

For many years I admired the carved elements that adorned 18th century furniture. I was in awe because I thought the shapes were beautiful, but I was frustrated because I could not figure out how to make them. In addition I thought that one had to be an artist to be able to carve and since I did not consider myself one, I thought that I would never be able to build the pieces that I admired so much. Through perseverance, education, dedication and hard work I have come to realize that carving is more of a learned skill than I thought.

I think that this is especially true when it comes to furniture embellishments and reproductions in particular. In the reproduction case there is an original to use as a model which is invaluable. Even with the original as a model there is a lot of learning and work to do, but it can be studied, analyzed and engineered so that it can be better understood and then with practice, increasingly good results can be achieved.

This book tries to help the reader analyze, understand and implement some specific motifs from antique originals. Emphasis is placed on analysis and understanding as well as specific details on how to render a shape and add the detail. It is my intent and hope that there is enough information that a patient and diligent reader can work from the text and complete each project to an acceptable level of success.

—*Tony Kubalak*
April 2010

Chapter 1
Cabriole Leg

The cabriole leg is one of the iconic motifs of 18th century furniture. It comes in many sizes from a 6-inch version on a bombé chest, a 30-inch one on a pier table, or a robust one that supports a high chest of drawers. In addition, the foot termination can also vary somewhat. The simplest termination is the pad foot. This is nothing more than a rounded foot with a circular pad underneath. A slightly more sophisticated version is called a slipper foot. This is more elongated and comes to a point in front. Moving up the sophistication scale is a trifid foot and, my favorite, the ball and claw foot. To further embellish the cabriole leg, builders will add a carved element to the knee. Typically, this could be a shell or a more sophisticated carving such as acanthus foliage. The combinations, though not infinite, are numerous.

This chapter will describe how to layout and shape a cabriole leg that is sized for a footstool or a chair. Foot termination will not be discussed here, but in a separate chapter. That chapter will describe in detail how to carve a ball and claw foot.

In all its various forms, the techniques used in shaping any cabriole leg are the same. In slightly over-simplified terms: A cabriole leg is shaped by making four bandsaw cuts, the same two cuts on two adjacent faces, and then rounding over the edges. There is a little more to it than that, but not much. So, if you keep this simplified picture in your mind as you work through the stages it will help you to better understand what is being accomplished at each step.

Before starting the layout there are a couple of things to consider in selecting the wood for the leg blank and the orientation of the template on the blank. First, use solid wood whenever possible. I know some people will advocate laminating three pieces of thinner stock to make this blank, but the lines formed by the joints will be very distracting to the eye. In addition, the amount of time and effort that I am going to put into this single piece of wood warrants the extra expense of employing solid stock. Second, if possible orient the grain of the cabriole leg so that, when viewed from the top, the growth rings are

concentric to the square post. This orientation will make a nice elliptical pattern on the knee of the leg. Figure 1-2 shows this orientation. Finally, in order to not end up with a leg that is too thin I use a thick pencil to trace the template. Then bandsaw to the outside of the pencil line. This leaves just enough stock so that after shaping, the leg is the correct size.

Any cabriole leg starts out as a cylindrical block of wood, typically with a 2¾–3 inch square cross-section. Since this leg is destined for a chair, the height of the leg is about 18-inches. Using the template in figure 1-1 transfer the pattern to the blank on two adjacent faces as shown in figure 1-3. At this point,

I would cut the mortises that will be needed to connect the rails. I find it much easier and better to cut the joints while the leg blank is square. I am not going to discuss cutting mortises here because that is not the focus of this chapter.

The next step is to bandsaw the leg blank to the template lines. Because there are patterns on two faces, one pattern will be removed when a cut is made on the adjacent surface. In addition, there may not be enough bearing surface that remains for the leg blank to sit properly on the bandsaw table. There are a couple of ways to deal with these problems. One is to make a cut the entire length and then tape the removed piece back in place. I have used this technique and it works fine. Another solution is to cut along a line and stop somewhere in the middle, back the piece out from the blade and make another cut along the same line but from the other end and stop just short of the first cut. In this manner the waste piece is not removed so the pattern is still there and the blank still has all the bearing surface that it needs. Figure 1-4 shows the results using this method. Once all of the template lines are to this point, complete the cut on

1-1 Cabriole leg template. If the template is not full size use the squares to align the two halves.

1-2 This is a top view of the leg blank. With the back post in the upper right hand corner the desired grain direction is as shown. If other constraints prohibit this orientation it is not that important.

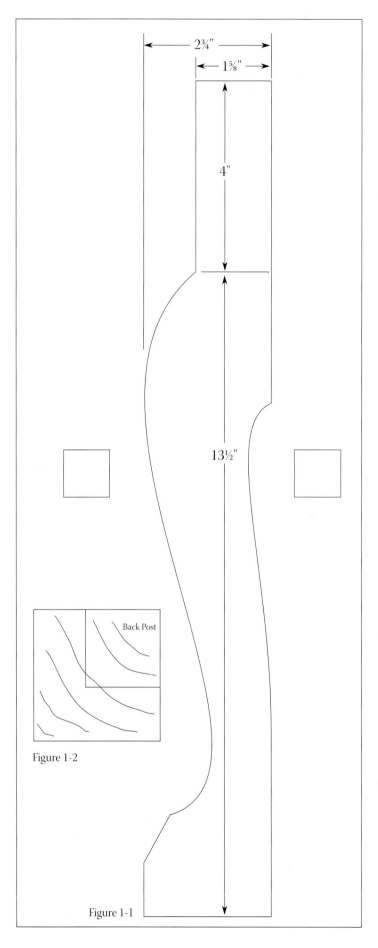

Figure 1-2

Back Post

Figure 1-1

2

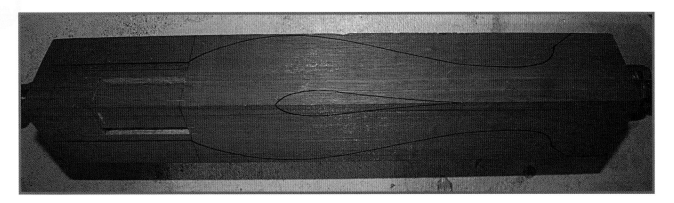

1-3 Transfer the leg template onto two adjacent faces of the blank.

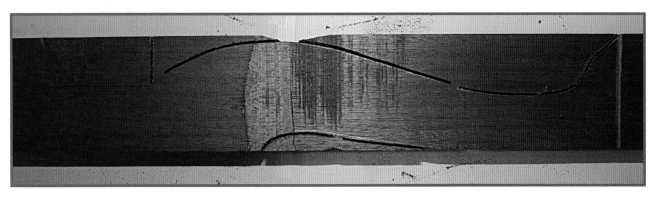

1-4 When working on the first face of the leg, bandsaw part way along from one direction and part way along from the other direction. Turn the blank 90° and cut the entire length of the lines.

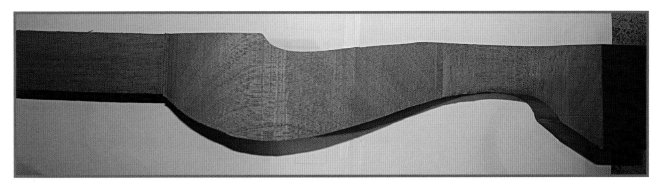

1-5 The cabriole leg after the bandsaw step.

each of them in turn. After the first piece of waste is removed, the lines to complete the cuts on the adjacent face are gone. However, the distance that remains to be cut is so small that you can do it by eye or a short pencil line can be easily drawn. Figure 1-5 shows the rough cabriole leg just after the bandsaw work

is complete. As you can see, it already looks a lot like the familiar cabriole shape.

The rest of the shaping of the leg is going to be done while the blank is securely clamped. The method I like best for holding a cabriole leg for shaping, or carving, is to put the leg

in an "I" beam clamp, which is then held in a machinists vice, which in turn is held in a woodworkers bench vice. In my bench-system, this puts the leg at a comfortable height so that I do not have to bend over too far. In addition, the leg is held very tight and it is easy to change the orientation of the leg as work progresses. Figure 1-10 shows my setup.

This next step is optional depending on the results of the bandsaw work. If the bandsaw cuts are accurate, straight and smooth, you can skip this cleanup step and go straight to the drawing on the layout lines. However, if the bandsaw work is a little rough, now is the time to touch it up a bit. With the leg secured, and one of the rougher faces pointing up, use a #49 patternmakers' rasp to straighten out any irregularities. The idea here is to get a more or less flat surface. This doesn't have to be perfect, just remove any divots and major ripples. Also, straighten the edge lines if they are severely crooked. This surface will still be rough, but it should be uniform. Repeat this process on the other surfaces that require this treatment.

The next stage is to round over the sharp corners. I start this process with a few layout lines. These are applied freehand. There will be four lines on each of the four faces. Start down at the ankle in the center. (Figure 1-6) Holding a pencil between your thumb and index finger, and with your other fingers as a guide, draw a line up towards the knee. This line is parallel to the outside edge and is half the ankle thickness inward. Figure 1-7 shows this line in place. Now starting at the same point as the first line, but using the back of the leg as the guide, draw a similar line. This second line is parallel to the back edge and half the ankle thickness inward. (Figure 1-8) Now, on the same face as the two previous lines, find a point halfway

1-6 Start at the ankle and draw one of the centerlines using your finger as guide.

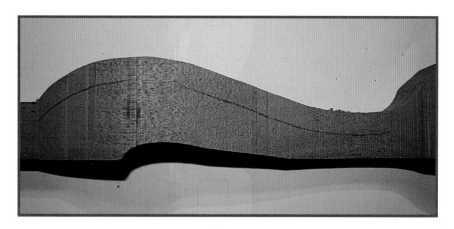

1-7 The first centerline after it is drawn up the leg. Note that this is not exactly a centerline, but it started out at the center in the ankle. This is really the extension of the centerline as measured from the front.

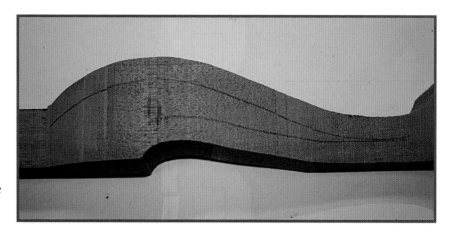

1-8 The extended centerline as measured from the back.

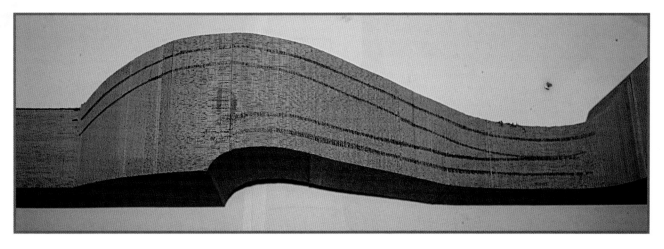

1-9 Draw a line halfway between the first lines and their respective edges.

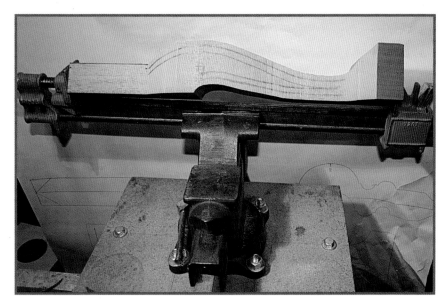

1-10 The leg is clamped and ready to be refined. Note that the machinists vise is attached to a board that is secured in the bench vise. This leaves the leg at a comfortable height.

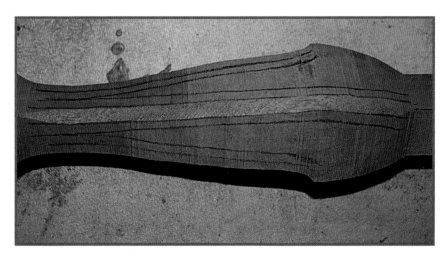

1-11 The first bevel cut is complete.

between one of the edges and its closest line, and in a similar manner as before draw another line parallel to that edge. Repeat for the other edge. This one face should now have four lines that are approximately parallel to their respective edges. (Figure 1-9) Repeat this process for the other three faces.

Now secure the leg to begin the refinement process. At this point, any cross-section of the leg is approximately square. After the next step, any cross-section will be an eight-sided figure. To achieve this, bevel each of the four-corners, from the knee to the ankle. Using the #49 flatten the section between the two lines closest to a given edge. Use the flat side of the #49 for the knee and wider portions. Then use the curved side for the ankle. Figure 1-11 shows the first bevel cut complete. Take care when rounding the knee to not hit the post. Also, note that because the foot has not yet been carved the ankle cannot be completely finished at this time. Repeat this operation for the other three edges. When doing the side edges stay a little distance away from the corner.

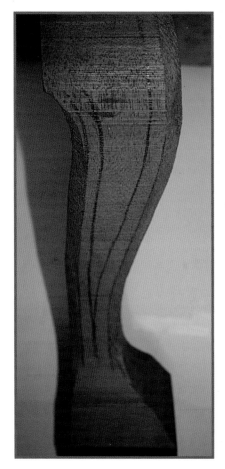

1-12 The corners are now removed. On the back edge, that is the side on the left, do not bevel the edge all the way to the end. Avoid the corner because a knee block will be attached later and this corner is going to be needed.

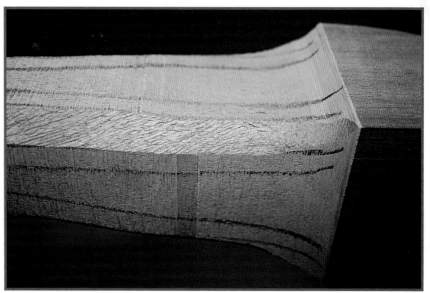

1-13 Remove the back corner all the way up.

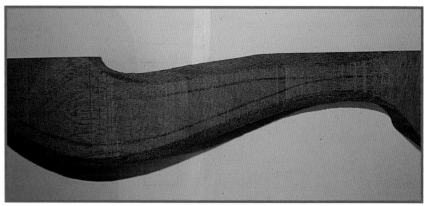

1-14 All four corners have been beveled.

This leg will eventually have a knee block attached and this point and line will be blended into that knee block. If too much wood is removed, too early, these two pieces cannot be blended well. Figure 1-12 shows this line in question. The back edge is a little different than the others in the way it terminates at the top. The goal here is blend the two surfaces so that they start at the lower post corner and continuously flow together. As part of this step, clean up the surface right up to the back of the post. Figure 1-13 shows the area and

treatment in question. Figure 1-14 shows the leg after all for edges have been beveled.

A similar series of cuts will now connect the inner most layout line with a line approximately centered in the beveled surface. Use the #49 for this also. Figure 1-15 shows early progress and figure 1-16 shows later progress. Keep in mind that the idea here is to get a smooth, round, surface the entire length of the leg. This is achieved by continuously adjusting the angle of the rasp as it is run from knee to ankle. In addition, vary

the pressure on the rasp depending on the surface. If the surface is relatively level, that is no divots or irregularities, use light pressure. If the surface is more uneven, use heavier pressure in those areas, lightening up as the pass completes.

At this point the surface should be uniform, round and even but rough. From now on, the shape of the leg will not change much, but the roughness will be smoothed. I use a bastard cut half round file for this operation. It is difficult to describe the smoothing operation in a series of discreet steps. Run the file up and down the leg removing all the facets while continually changing the angle pressure used. The surface should be continuous to the touch and your hand should not feel any hills or valleys when moving in any, and all, directions. After the file has removed the rasp marks, you can use a smooth cut file, or sandpaper, or both. It depends on how smooth you want the surface. I have used both and I usually end up with 120-grit sandpaper. Figure 1-17 shows the completed, shaped cabriole leg.

1-15 Blend the centerline extensions on the adjacent faces into the center of the bevel edge just created. The successive beveling will approximate rounding in a symmetric way.

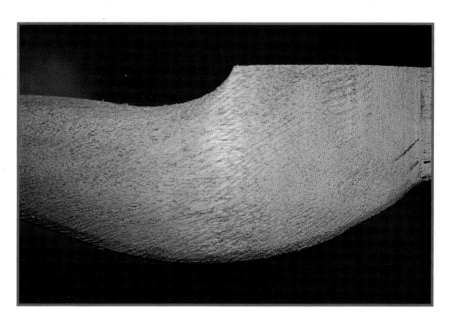

1-16 As the guidelines are removed, continue to blend the facets to form a uniform and continuous surface. Remove any irregularities remaining from the saw cuts.

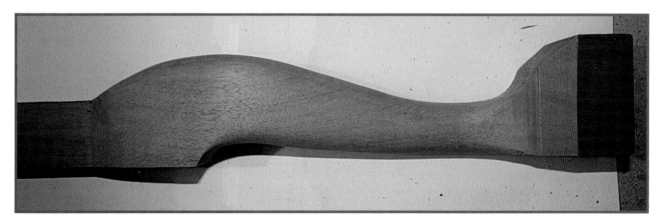

1-17 Clean up the file marks with a smooth cut file or sandpaper. The leg is now ready for foot and knee carving.

Chapter 2
Philadelphia Style Ball and Claw Foot

The ball and claw foot is a very elegant and dramatic termination for a cabriole leg. It became very popular in 18th century American furniture and reached its peak in the third quarter of that century. The ball and claw foot is probably most often associated with what are commonly called Chippendale pieces, but it is also often found on Queen Anne pieces. The facing page shows some typical examples of furniture graced with ball and claw feet.

Many people probably think that there is only one version of a ball and claw foot, and that one is just like another. But there are at least 4 visually distinct varieties, each with its own unique characteristics. The differences vary by where a particular piece was made, with Philadelphia, Boston, Newport, RI and New York being the regional centers. Some of the differences are subtle, but others rather obvious. One of the variations is the open talon. This is a characteristic unique to pieces made in Newport, although not every foot carved by a Newport cabinetmaker had open talons. Swept-back side toes are characteristic of a foot carved in Boston. Vertical toes, symmetrically located in the four-corners of the blank, are characteristic of a foot carved in Philadelphia; It is the Philadelphia style foot that I am going to describe in this chapter.

At first, it might seem quite intimidating and maybe almost impossible to extract a decent looking ball and claw foot from a blank of wood. I say that because that is how I felt about it once upon a time. I thought that a person had to be an artist to be able to sculpt such a refined element. However, I learned a method that describes the foot in measurable, repeatable and deterministic steps. This method transferred the artistry into engineering and the engineering is then implemented as a series of steps. I did not invent this method, but I do understand it; It is this method that I am going to describe here.

Before I begin there are a couple of other preliminary yet very important points to make. You might not appreciate these points until you have carved several feet, but the more you do appreciate them the better you will understand how to

carve the foot and the better the results you will get. I like to separate carving a ball and claw foot, or any carving for that matter, into two big categories. One is what to carve, and the other is the actual carving. Once you know what to carve, then all it takes is practice to make your hands do what your mind, and eye, tell you. However, if you do not know what to carve you will make random cuts and wonder in frustration why it is not looking like it should. This method of carving a ball and claw foot is as much about understanding what to carve as it is about carving it. In fact, once you understand the method the actual carving is almost secondary.

Since the foot that I am going to describe in this chapter is the termination of a cabriole leg, I am going to assume the leg has been cut, shaped and that it is well understood. The foot begins with some layout,

Ball and Claw Foot Layout Diagrams

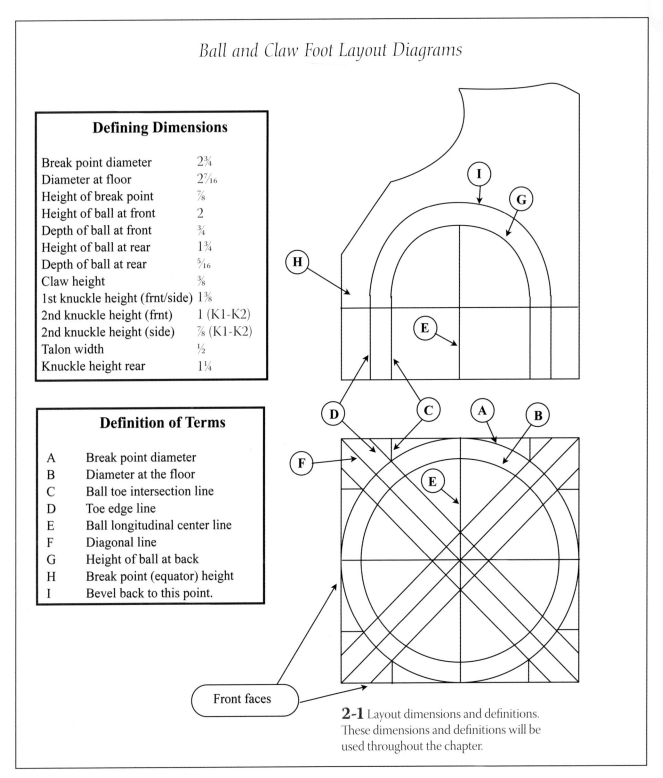

Defining Dimensions

Break point diameter	2¾
Diameter at floor	2⁷⁄₁₆
Height of break point	⅞
Height of ball at front	2
Depth of ball at front	¾
Height of ball at rear	1¾
Depth of ball at rear	⁵⁄₁₆
Claw height	⅜
1st knuckle height (frnt/side)	1⅜
2nd knuckle height (frnt)	1 (K1-K2)
2nd knuckle height (side)	⅞ (K1-K2)
Talon width	½
Knuckle height rear	1¼

Definition of Terms

A	Break point diameter
B	Diameter at the floor
C	Ball toe intersection line
D	Toe edge line
E	Ball longitudinal center line
F	Diagonal line
G	Height of ball at back
H	Break point (equator) height
I	Bevel back to this point.

Front faces

2-1 Layout dimensions and definitions. These dimensions and definitions will be used throughout the chapter.

actually a lot of layout. It is important to not only get the layout lines on the blank correct, but to understand why they are there. Because of the engineering nature of this process, a series of measurements completely defines the foot. Figure 2-1 lists the set of measurements that define this foot. The layout starts on the bottom of the blank. Draw in the two diagonal lines connecting opposite corners and locate the center of the blank. With this as the center, use a divider to scribe two concentric circles. One with the break point dimension as the diameter and the other with the "diameter at the floor" dimension. Use a 0.5mm mechanical pencil to highlight these circles. Figure 2-2 shows these lines. Next, draw two lines parallel to each of the diagonal lines, ¼-inch on either side of the diagonals. These lines will place and define the width of the claws and talons. Figure 2-3 shows these lines. Using a square, draw a line perpendicular to each of the four faces of the blank through the center. These lines will be extended up the faces of the block and will locate the longitudinal center of the four sides of the ball. Now use a square to draw the lines labeled "C" in figure 2-1. These lines will be transferred onto the two back faces and are the left and right limits of the ball segment on that face. Figure 2-4 shows the complete layout on the foot bottom. Now that the layout is complete on the bottom of the foot the next step is to transfer some of the dimensions from the bottom onto the faces of the blank and add a few others.

Using a square, transfer each of the lines from the bottom up the faces of each of the four sides. Figure 2-5 shows these various lines. Now, draw a line parallel to the bottom ⅞-inch up from the bottom on each of the four faces. I will refer to this line as the break point. This is the horizontal centerline of the ball, or in geographical terms, the equator. Figure 2-6 shows these lines. On the two back faces, locate the point "G" from figure 2-1. This is the height of the ball at the rear. With a compass, draw a semi-circle that goes through point "G" and is tangent to the two limit lines at the break point as illustrated in figure 2-1. Figure 2-7 shows this on the leg blank. The layout for the back face is now complete. There are two layout items remaining on

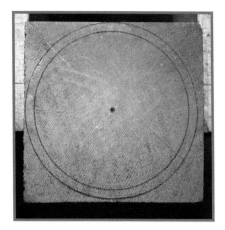

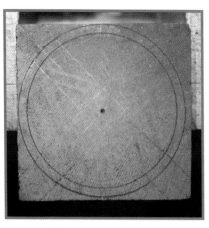

2-2 The larger circle is the diameter of the ball and the smaller circle is the diameter of the ball at the floor. The diameter of the ball will occur at the break point ⅞ inches up from the floor. Note that the circles were scribed with a divider and then traced with a pencil. The scribed circle is used so that a crisp line will remain after carving.

each of the front faces. These will locate the height of the ball in front and the depth of the ball in front.

Draw the front ball height as a horizontal line on the front two faces. Finally, we need to locate the point that is the intersection of three mutually perpendicular planes. This point is buried in the blank at this stage and is not visible. The object of this discussion is to understand how to locate this point so that we can carve to reveal it. When the foot is carved this will be the top of the ball in the front measured along the vertical centerline of the ball and it will be buried inside the blank the distance designated by the "depth of the ball in front" dimension. This is the most difficult and obscure concept of all of the ball and claw defining dimensions. You will need to think about this awhile before you fully appreciate how to visualize and locate it.

2-3 The two lines parallel to each of the diagonals define the width and placement of the toes.

2-4 This is the complete layout on the bottom of the foot. Note the centerlines and perpendicular transfers to where the toes meet the ball.

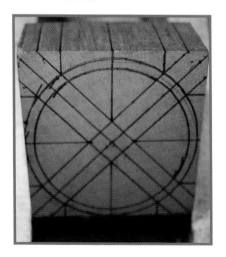

2-5 Transfer the lines from the bottom onto each of the four faces of the foot. These will be used for further layout.

11

2-6 The "break point" line is ⅞ inches up from, and parallel to, the floor. This is the widest part of the ball. In geographical terms, this is the equator.

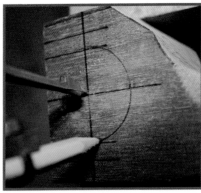

2-7 The layout of the ball on each of the back faces. Note how the semi-circular arc of the ball blends into the lines that are the intersection of the toe at the surface of the ball.

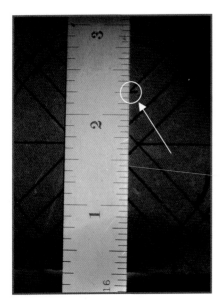

2-8 The layout mark showing the depth of the ball in front. This is measured from the outer circle on the front face.

To locate this point we need to use the square portion of the base of the foot and the bottom of the foot. On the bottom of the blank start from the outer circle on one of the front faces and measure back the distance specified by the "depth of the ball in front" along the diameter. Make this with a pencil. Figure 2-8 shows this location. Now we need to transfer this line to the top of the blank. Use

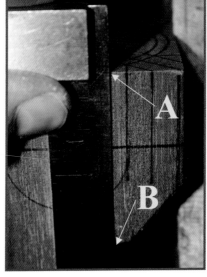

2-9 Use a square to transfer the "depth of the ball distance" to the top of the blank. That is transferred from point A to point B.

a square to transfer the line from the bottom of the foot up the back face. Figure 2-9 shows this transfer. Figure 2-10 shows this distance transferred up the side and onto the top surface. The red line on top shown in figure 2-10 is directly on top of the "depth of the ball in front" line first drawn on the bottom of the blank. Now on the front face extend the vertical centerline so that it intersects the

line just drawn on top. Figure 2-11 shows a technique for extending the centerline by setting a depth gauge, or an adjustable square, to the desired length. This intersection point is directly above the hidden point we are trying to find. Think of drilling straight at this point to the horizontal plane determined by the "height of the ball in front" dimension. This is the buried point we are trying to locate. Figure 2-12 shows the intersection of the two lines together with the horizontal height line. Imagine where the vertical line through the intersection point meets the horizontal plane. That is the point in question. Now repeat this process for the other front face. The layout is now complete and it is time to start removing wood.

This starts with making a few saw cuts that will establish the toes. The front toe and the two side toes are sawed their entire length down to the depth of the break point diameter. Only the bottom half of the back toe can be sawed on each side, otherwise the back webbing would be impacted. Figure 2-13 shows how to clamp the leg in position for sawing the front and side toes and figure 2-14 shows how to saw the back toes. This sawing operation is very beneficial for two reasons. First it will make the carving easier and second it is much less likely to damage the toe during carving.

The strategy for carving the foot is to first separate the ball from the toes, then shape the ball, then refine the toes and finally establish the claws. The ball is formed by four separate segments, which the eye

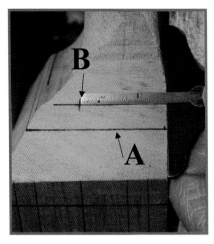

2-10 Finally, transfer this distance to the top surface as shown. This line is the deepest part of the ball in front. The point of interest is at the intersection of the red line on top and the extension of the centerline.

2-11 To help transfer the centerline to the line on the top of the blank, set a depth gauge to the desired length as shown. Use the same reference face to mark the centerline on the top of the blank.

2-12 Extend the longitudinal center of the ball so that it intersects the horizontal line just drawn. This is point B. This intersection point is very important in locating the ultimate point that will become the top of the ball. In fact, the ultimate top of the ball is directly below this intersection point at the height specified by the "height of the ball in front" dimension, which is the line, labeled A.

2-13 Saw down to the break point diameter on both sides of the front and two side toes. These saw cuts isolate the toes so they are much better protected from damage when establishing the ball surfaces.

connects to give the illusion of a continuous surface. First, work on one of these four segments and then go to the other three in turn. Start with a back one, although it doesn't matter whether you start with the

front or the back. Because carving is a subtractive process, one segment of the ball will start out as a part of a cylinder. The cylinder will be formed first. Since the top of the ball at the back is completely hidden the first thing to do is establish this top surface. With a #5, 12mm gouge, make a stop cut straight down following the semi-circular arc that was drawn on the back face. This is the arc labeled "G" in figure 2-1. Figure 2-15 shows how to start. With the same #5, bevel back into this stop cut along the entire length of the arc. Using figure 2-1 as a guide look at the line formed by the arc "I" and the straight line "D". Also, look at the line formed by the arc "G" and the straight line "C". The "G" line represents the stop cut line and the "I" line represents the line where the bevel cut into the "G" will start. This is the result of this step and it will not be made in one cut but rather a series of cuts. Iteratively, deepen the stop cut and bevel back until

the depth reaches that given by the dimension "depth of ball at rear." I use a depth gauge to measure progress for this as shown in figure 2-16. Figure 2-17 shows the intermediate progress and figure 2-18 shows this step complete.

The top of the cylinder is done. Now form the cylinder between the toes by rounding over this segment to match the outer most circle from the bottom of the foot. In figure 2-19 the red area is to be removed. Feather the bevel cuts made at the top of the arc into the saw cuts made on the sides of the toes. It is important to not cut into the toe surface defined by the saw cut, but rather to blend that surface into the angled one behind the arc. Note that the centerline of this segment will remain high. Figures 2-20 through 2-23 show this process. Use a flat

2-14 Because the ball is not open on the top on the back faces, the saw can only be used to isolate the bottom half. If the saw were used to isolate the top half of the toe, it would cut into the webbing and ankle.

2-15 With a #5, 12mm gouge begin to establish the ball on one of the back faces by setting in along the semi-circular arc as shown.

2-16 Use a depth gauge set to the "depth of the ball in back" dimension to know when to stop carving. There still is a little more to go.

2-17 The desired depth is reached by iteratively setting in along the semi-circular arc and beveling back into this cut. This figure shows intermediate progress.

chisel, as shown, and a gouge to blend the bevel cuts into the sides of the toes. I used a ¾-inch, flat bench chisel, for this operation. The size is not particularly important, but I feel more comfortable with a little bigger one. I also find that I have more control with a flat chisel that I would with a gouge.

The break point line has been mostly removed. Redraw this line by hand or with a ruler. Figure 2-24 shows this line redrawn. At this point, there is a rounded, cylindrical surface, with a rounded top. Form the top of the ball by rounding over the top edge down to the depth previously established. I use the ⅜-inch, flat, bench chisel for this operation. The break point line will remain high and the surface will fall off smoothly towards the top. Figure 2-25 shows the beginning of this process, and figure 2-26 shows the top half of the ball complete.

Now, move to the bottom half of the ball. Because this portion of the cylinder is still connected to the toes, I will have to separate them as I go. Start with a flat chisel resting on the saw cut surface of one of the adjacent toes and make a cut into

2-18 Here the final depth has been reached.

2-19 Remove the material above the outer circle, and between the toes, following the circular arc. This will form a cylinder and it is the next step in shaping the ball.

2-20 Use a ⅜-inch flat, chisel to form the cylinder. Be mindful of the grain and change directions as needed. Here is early progress.

2-21 More progress forming the cylinder.

2-22 Blend the side of the toe into the surface formed by beveling into the top of the cylinder with a #5 gouge.

2-23 Here the cylinder is complete. The next steps will round over the top and bottom halves to form part of a sphere.

the cylinder, parallel to the toe side surface. It is very important that the chisel back be flat against the toe side. This will insure that the cut is going in the correct direction. It is easy to accidentally cut into this toe surface which will translate into undercut toes which are undesirable. Figure 2-27 shows registering the back of the flat chisel against the toe side and the direction of the cut. Note that this cut will follow the line "D" on the bottom as shown in figure 2-2. After making the flat chisel cut, carve off the bottom edge into this cut. Figure 2-28 shows this technique and early progress. Repeat these cuts down to the inner circle as viewed from the bottom. Analogous to the top half, keep the break

2-24 Redraw the break point line in preparation to forming the top of the ball.

point line high and round down continuously to the inner circle along the entire length between the two toes. Use the technique described above to separate the ball from the second toe. Figure 2-29 shows this step complete. This is the point where using the divider to

2-25 Form the top half of the ball by rounding the semi-circular arc down to the depth established earlier. Begin by cutting the top edge with a ⅜-inch flat chisel. As the top of the ball nears the desired depth, start the cuts closer and closer to the break point line. Remember the break point line is the high portion of this section and the surface falls off from there.

2-26 The top half of the ball is now complete. Strive for a smooth, crisp line where the ball meets the web on top and the toes on the sides.

2-27 Round the bottom of the ball using a ⅜-inch, flat chisel. Be careful not to cut the corners of the chisel into the toes. Rest the back of the chisel against one of the toes and press down to make a stop cut. Make this cut deep at the bottom and shallower as the break point nears. Carve along the surface of the ball into these stop cuts.

2-28 The bottom edge is removed down to the arc specified by the inner circle. Note how the corners next to the toes are cut down almost to the inner circle. The breakpoint line is still visible and remains high.

score the inner circle on the bottom makes a difference. It is easier, and more exact, to get a nice crisp line when carving to a scored line than to a pencil line. At this point one quarter of the ball has been formed. It is probably a little rough, with many facets left from using the flat chisel. These will be removed with a file and sandpaper.

Now that the first segment of the ball has been carved, clean up the surface with a small, half round file. The goal here is to smooth this segment to be part of a sphere. With the flat portion of the file, smooth the surface of the ball in all directions while continuously altering the angle of the file. Vary the pressure depending on the surface texture and contour. As a final smoothing operation take a small bit of 120 grit sandpaper, and with your finger as support, move over the entire surface of the ball until it is smooth, continuous, and uniform. (Figure 2-30) Repeat these operations on the other back face. Figure 2-31 shows both of the back faces of the ball complete.

2-29 The bottom half of the ball is now established. It still has many facets that will be removed later. Note that the surface of the toes is extended as the bottom of the cylinder is removed.

Now, work on one of the front sections of the ball. The front sections are a little less work because the top of the ball is more exposed and the toes were completely separated from the ball with the saw cuts. So, start by rounding the section to conform to the outer circle as drawn on the bottom of the foot. (Figure 2-32)

2-30 Use a small file to smooth the facets left by the chisel. Continuously vary the pressure and angle of the file to form a uniform and smooth surface.

As with the back surfaces, I use a ⅜-inch, flat chisel.

The next step is to uncover the hidden point that I talked about earlier. This is the top of the ball, some distance into the blank. If the "height of the ball in front" horizontal line has been carved away, redraw it. Also, sketch in a curved line that connects

2-31 Both of the back ball segments are complete. Note that the two spherical surfaces should appear to be on a surface interrupted by the back toe.

2-32 Now move to one of the front sections. First, form a cylinder, as was done in the back using a ⅜-inch, flat chisel. One of the front portions of the cylinder is complete.

2-33 Draw an arc connecting the inside surfaces of the toes and the intersection point drawn earlier.

2-34 Use a ⅜-inch, flat chisel to form a horizontal line at the ball height line between the toes. Be careful not to dig the corners of the chisel into the toe sides. These can be almost impossible to remove if they are too deep. Use a #9, 15mm gouge to cut vertically down from the intersection point to the horizontal surface just established.

2-35 Using a #7 gouge, blend this surface into each of the toe surfaces. The top of the ball height is now established by the horizontal surface and the depth is set by the curved surface.

the inside surfaces of the toes and passes through the depth point. (Figure 2-33) With a flat chisel set in along this line. Be careful as the corners of the chisel get close to the toes because they can dig into the toe sides and these can be difficult, if not impossible, to remove. You can get aggressive in the middle of the ball though. Figure 2-34 shows

what I mean. Now use a #9, 15mm gouge and remove material between the toes down to the ball height line. The goal is to carve to the curved line sketched in earlier and with a nice smooth surface connect the inside surfaces of the toes to the depth point down to the height line. A #7, 16mm gouge gives a good transition curve when blending into the

toe surfaces. Figure 2-35 shows the operation complete. At this point, there should be a continuous surface connecting the inside faces of the toes and a flat horizontal ledge in between. Now redraw the breakpoint line if needed and round the top and bottom of the ball using the same techniques as were used on the back segments. Remember not to undercut the toes! Figures 2-36 through 2-39 show how to shape the top half. Repeat this process for the other front face. Figure 2-40 shows the front two segments complete.

As is typical of a Philadelphia ball and claw foot, the ball is slightly higher in front than in back. If things have gone well, your eye should be able to sense a continuous spherical surface when sighting the front section and back section together. Figure 2-41 shows this continuous surface.

It is now time to work on the toes. The front and back toes are straight forward, and there is one extra step to the side toes. Work on the back

17

2-36 Begin to separate the toes and the ball by using a flat chisel registered against the side of the toe. This will prevent undercutting the toe.

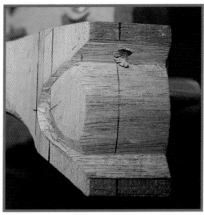

2-37 Intermediate progress. The toes are starting to emerge.

2-38 Start to round the top half of the ball.

2-39 The top of the ball is now established and the vertical circular surface is blended into the inner surfaces of the toes on both sides. The bottom half of the ball is formed with the same techniques as before.

2-40 Carve the other front face in the same manner. Note how the two portions of the ball appears to be one continuous surface with the toe on top.

2-41 When complete the four segments of the ball should appear as one surface interrupted by the toes. In addition, the visible part of the ball should fall off going from front to back. This is the desired visual effect.

toe first. The webbing between the back toe and the adjacent side toes needs to be excavated and blended. This will further define each toe so that detail can be added. Using a #7, 16mm or a #5, 12 mm, gouge gently blend the ankle into the top of the ball. The depth should not be increased so feather the cuts so that no material is removed right at the top of the ball. As you feather the web up the ankle, also extend the blending to include the side surfaces of the toes. It is somewhat of a judgement call as to how far up the ankle to take this, but a generous 2 inches or so is typical. Figure 2-42 shows the result of this operation. It is a good idea to do this step on both sides of the back toe before moving to detail it. Both sides of the toe need to be fully defined or detailing it will not work. Figure 2-43 show both sides of the back toe complete.

Notice that each toe is in one corner of the original square. Thus, there is a sharp corner running down its center. This needs to be removed. When viewed from the bottom visualize the triangle formed by the corner. Remove this triangle using the #49 rasp. Figure 2-44 shows the triangle. What remains is a rectangular tube. (Figure 2-45) This needs to be turned into a semi-circular tube. I use a ½-inch, flat chisel for most of this and clean up the facets with a file. (Figure 2-46)

2-42 Establish the web on the back faces by blending the ankle surface into the area just above the ball. In addition, blend it into the toes on each side. One portion of the back web is complete. Note how the surfaces from the toes blend and flow together into the ankle and around the ball.

Now mark the claw height. Using the claw height dimension, make a mark at this distance measured up from the bottom on the circular tube. Carry this line around the perimeter of the tube. Figure 2-47 shows this line. With a flat chisel, the bevel side facing the bottom of the foot, score along the perimeter line just drawn. Figure 2-48 shows this cut. From the bottom side of this stop cut, pare away the tube into it along the entire length of the cut. A couple of light passes should give a suitable depth. Figure 2-49 shows this step. This lower segment will become the claw.

In this claw segment use a flat chisel and make a convex ramp from the top of the tube down to the inner circle on the bottom of the foot. Do this in multiple passes and take care not to cut past the inner circle. I want the claw to end right at edge of this circle. Figure 2-50 shows the ramp. The claw is going

2-43 The other back portion of the web is now complete. The middle section is isolated and will be refined into the back toe and claw.

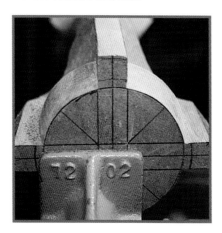

2-45 Now that the triangle is gone, a rectangular tube remains. Refine this into a circular tube using a ⅜-inch, flat chisel.

to be a relatively narrow pyramid that comes to a point at the bottom of the foot. Sketch in a centerline down the ramp. Using a flat chisel begin to remove the lower corners of the ramp on either side of the centerline. (Figure 2-51) Round over the ridge of the claw slightly, using the chisel as a scraper. Blend the rounded spine into the sides. Figure 2-52 shows the completed claw.

Now make a mark up the back tube using the dimension "height of knuckle in back." With the round

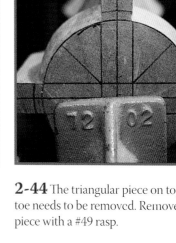

2-44 The triangular piece on top of the toe needs to be removed. Remove this piece with a #49 rasp.

2-46 Cleanup the circular tube with a file and/or sandpaper.

2-47 Use the claw height dimension as measured from the bottom to draw a line on the surface of the circular tube.

2-48 Cut straight down on this line with a flat chisel. Note that the bevel side of the chisel is facing the bottom of the foot.

2-49 From the bottom side cut into the stop cut just made. This is going to lower the claw a bit from the toe above it.

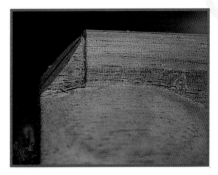

2-50 With a flat chisel make a ramp from the top of the toe to inner circle on the bottom of the foot. Leave a slight arc in the ramp to give a little curvature to the claw. Note that the tip of the claw will end on the inner circle at the bottom. Be careful not to cut into this circle.

2-51 The claw is going to be a pyramid with the wide portion near the toe and the point at the bottom. Cut off the corners on each side as shown. Make several light cuts as opposed to one or two heavy cuts. The results will be much better. The rough pyramid that is the claw is now complete. Round over the sharp edges using the edge of a flat chisel as a scraper.

2-52 The claw is complete.

2-53 (BELOW) To form the knuckle, first draw a line at the dimension "height of knuckle in back." Use the #49 rasp to make a semi-circular depression centered just above this line. Go to a depth of a little less that ¼-inch. This is not critical, so measure by eye.

side of the #49 rasp, create a semi-circular depression centered just above the mark just made. Carve to a depth of about ³⁄₁₆ inch–¼ inch to start. (Figure 2-53) With a #5, 12mm gouge, narrow the tube on each side centered on the rasp cut just made. This is going to thin the ankle and give it some tension. (Figure 2-54) Using the small file, round over the ridges just made and blend, and smooth, all of the surfaces together. These don't have to be perfect at this point because they will get touched up later.

The toe segment just above the claw will be shaped in a similar manner. With a #49 rasp make a slight depression along the spine of the toe (Figure 2-55). Don't make this too deep or the segment won't look right. Narrow the sides with the #5, 12mm gouge as before. (Figure 2-56) File and sand the ridges to form a uniform and smooth surface. Figure 2-57 shows the finished toe segment.

Before work can begin on the remaining toes, form the web between them. Scooping out between them and leaving a slight step down to the

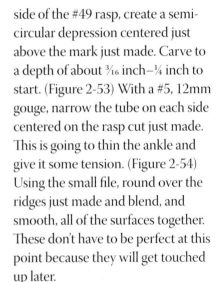

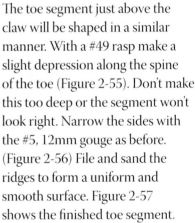

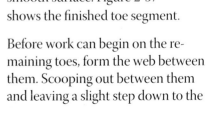

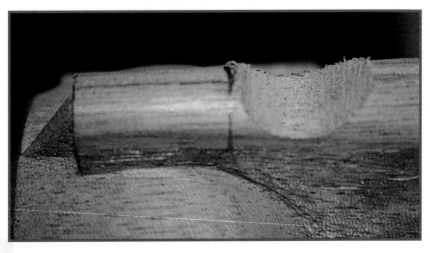

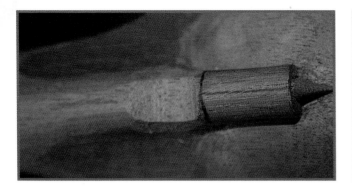

2-54 To add a little tension to the ankle, thin out each side at the center of the depression formed earlier. Use a #5, 12mm gouge for this operation. Here the ankle has been thinned. Use a small half-round file to round the corners and blend and smooth the surface.

2-55 With the #49 rasp, make a slight concave cut in the top of the toe segment.

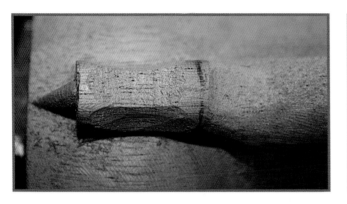

2-56 Thin out the sides with the #5 gouge in the same manner as previously shown.

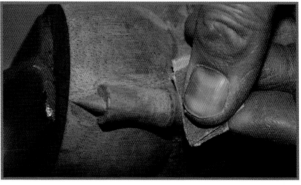

2-57 Finally, use sandpaper backed by your finger to complete the toe surface.

ball will form the web between the front toe, and one of the side toes. This step is approximately ¹⁄₁₆ inch, but is measured by eye. Draw guide lines as shown in figure 2-58 to define the web. Use a #9, 13mm gouge to scoop out the material between the toes. Taper the cut to feather out at the top of the guideline. The goal is to form steep ridge lines that will establish and extend the toes up into the ankle. Figure 2-59 shows significant progress in forming the web. As the web is nearing completion use a smaller #9 to form a vertical wall between the toe and the web. This will give nice definition to each toe and show tension when complete. Figure 2-60 shows the technique and figure 2-61 shows the web complete.

I want the web to be a smooth surface between the toes so I use flatter gouges to smooth the ridges left by the #9's. When the carving is done, there are many little facets on the surface. I clean these up with scrapers. I have a set of scrapers with semi-circular tips of various radii. These work great for cleaning up the web and blending the transitions into the toes and ankle. Complete the web on the other side before moving to the front toe.

Now that the webs are complete it is time to work on the front toe. The same techniques are used to form the front toe as were used to form the back one with the exception that there are more segments. However,

each segment is shaped and refined in the same way. Remove the triangular ridge using the #49 rasp to form the rectangular tube. Round over the edges to form a semi-circular tube. Form the claw in the same manner as in the back. Figure 2-62 shows this complete. Mark the "first knuckle height" and the "second knuckle height" around the perimeter of the tube. These numbers will probably not align with the angles from the bandsaw. Figure 2-63 shows this situation. Place the numbers as described, and then with a flat chisel connect the knuckle lines with a straight segment. (Figure 2-64) Round over the edges to re-establish the semi-circular tube. Figure 2-65 shows the front toe

21

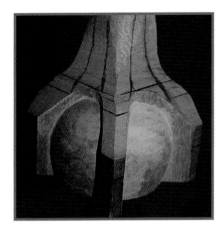

2-58 Sketch guidelines for the web between the front and side toes. Try to keep the width of each toe uniform as the web moves up the ankle. Define the web using a series of # 9 gouges. Feather the cuts into the ankle according to the guidelines.

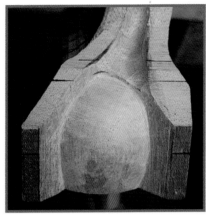

2-59 Note the steep walls along the toe sides as the web is formed. These are necessary because they will become the extension of the toes into the ankle.

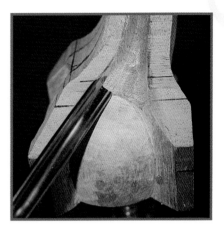

2-60 Strive for a nearly vertical wall from the toe down to the web. Use a smaller, #9 gouge, pressed against the toe side and cut parallel to the toe.

2-61 The web is now established. Smooth the surface with flatter gouges, scrapers and sandpaper.

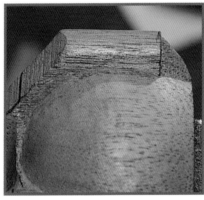

2-62 Remove the triangle on top of the front toe. A #49 rasp removes the triangle and forms a rectangular tube. Form a semi-circular tube just as on the back. Form the claw as before.

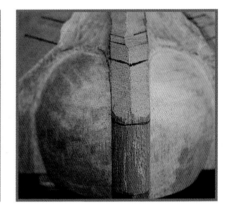

2-63 The angles formed by the bandsaw cuts will probably not align with the knuckle heights. The pencil lines are the correct heights.

2-64 Draw in the desired heights and connect these lines with a flat chisel.

2-65 Re-establish the semi-circular tube with the new knuckle placements.

reshaped with the proper knuckle heights and rounded as needed.

Starting from the bottom, work on one segment at a time. With the round face of a #49 rasp make a slight concave depression centered in the toe segment as shown in figure 2-66. With the #5, 12mm gouge, thin out both sides of the segment as was done on the back toe. Using the small half round file round over the ridges, smooth and blend the surfaces as before. Repeat this process

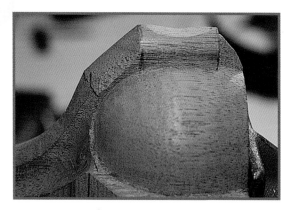

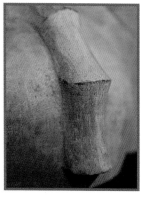

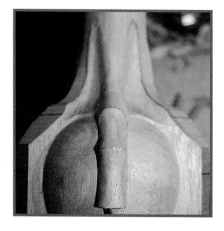

2-66 Start to detail each segment of the toe by beginning with a slight depression cut using a small half round file or the #49 rasp. As was done on the back toe, thin out each side of the segment using a #5, 12mm gouge. As before smooth and blend the surfaces using a small file. Sometimes a chisel helps to give a nice crisp edge to the knuckles.

2-67 Strive to get a crisp, straight ridge line at the intersection of two toe segments. This shows attention to detail and will enhance the look.

2-68 Finally, blend the top segment into the ankle.

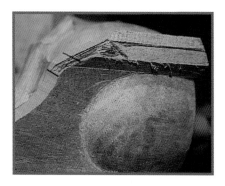

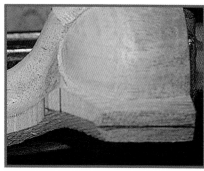

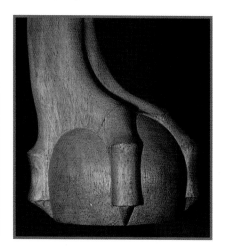

2-69 The side toes come next. Remove the shaded area with a #49 rasp.

2-70 The shaded area is gone. Note that the centerline of the segment will be a ridge. Once the previous step is complete, form and detail the segments as before.

2-71 The ball and claw foot is now complete!

on the next segment up the toe. Pay particular attention the ridge line between two segments. Strive for a crisp and straight line. This is a sign of attention to detail and fine craftsmanship. Figure 2-67 shows two segments complete. Finally, there is the transition segment into the ankle. This is just rounded and does not have the depression or the thinning cuts. Figure 2-68 shows the completed front toe.

The side toes are all that is left to complete the ball and claw foot. The only difference in forming a side toe

is one cut with the rasp in the second segment that will transition the toe into the ankle. Once that is done, placing the claw and segments, and refining them, is the same as on the front toe. Figure 2-69 shows the side toe before being reshaped. With the #49 rasp remove the shaded area to end up with the result shown in figure 2-70. Now proceed as before. Figure 2-71 shows the completed foot.

This foot is not a simple shape to develop and it will take some study and practice to get comfortable with

the techniques and method. If your expectation is that you will read this description once and then be able to carve a perfect foot you will be disappointed. However, if you study the method and work to understand it and then have patience and practice the techniques you will end up with increasingly pleasing results. I have been carving this foot with this method for ten years and I still find ways to perfect my technique. I love this motif and I look forward to carving it every chance that I get.

Chapter 3
Shell on Knee Carving

A shell carved on the knee of a leg is a motif that was popular during the Queen Anne period. It is an advanced embellishment from earlier motifs, but less refined than acanthus arrangements that adorned later Chippendale pieces. Although the shell is a rather simple design, it adds a significant step up in elegance to the piece.

The shell motif that this chapter will describe is carved from the solid into the knee of a cabriole leg. The design of the shell is one that was common on 18th century Philadelphia furniture. It is most often found on chairs, but I have seen it on desks, dressing tables and others. The facing page shows some common applications.

Before a shell can be carved on the knee of a cabriole leg, that leg has to be fully shaped and smoothed. This chapter assumes that has been done and will start with that as a given. Begin by making a template of the shell profile from figure 3-1. I use boxboard to make templates, but Mylar also is a good choice. Match the curves of the shell with the gouges available by cutting the template with the carving tools. Now trace around the template onto the shaped cabriole leg. Center the shell on the knee approximately ¾ of an inch down from the shoulder line. The shell should be sized so that it fills the vast majority of the knee without spilling onto the knee blocks. Figure 3-2 shows typical placement of the shell on the knee. Figure 3-3 shows the template transferred to the knee.

Now that the profile has been drawn on the leg, the shell is raised from the surface by lowering the background around it. Making perpendicular stop cuts around the entire perimeter of the shell does this. Then relief cuts are feathered into them. The stop cuts should be perpendicular to the surface so the angle of the tool will change because the surface curvature changes around the shell. Use a variety of gouges and match the shape of the gouge to that of the curves of the shell. Conceptually this is a simple process, but it takes some time to make your way around the entire perimeter. Figures 3-4 and 3-5 show some early progress. Typically I will make a few stop cuts and then feather in the relief cuts instead of stop cutting around the entire perimeter first. The second option works

perfectly well and it is completely up to the carver. To reduce the number of times you have to change tools make as many cuts with one as possible before putting it down.

When feathering in the relief cut, stay close to the stop cut at first. Later smooth any ridges or irregularities with a chisel or file. End up smoothing with a file or 120-grit sandpaper. Figure 3-6 shows the entire shell "raised" above the surface of the knee. Figure 3-7 shows the operation completed.

The shell is now ready for detailing. Note that the only difference between this shell and the applied shell discussed in another chapter is that this one does not have the wings on either side of the root. First, draw in the ray lines that will separate the lobes. From the template, mark

Philadelphia Style Carved Shell on a Cabriole Leg Knee

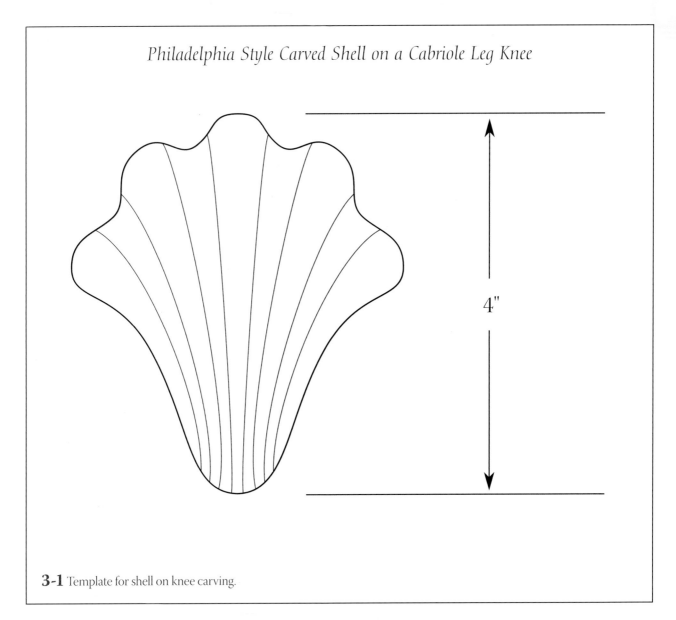

4"

3-1 Template for shell on knee carving.

3-2 Center the template ¾ of an inch below the post.

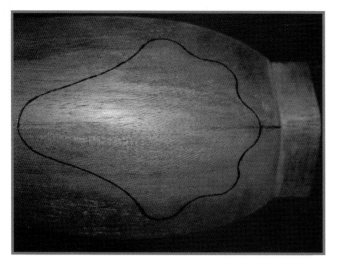

3-3 The shell transferred onto the knee.

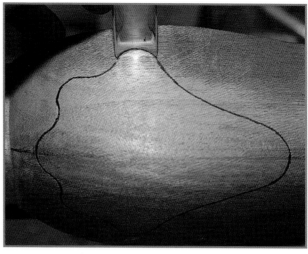

3-4 Early progress setting in around the perimeter of the shell. The set in cuts should be perpendicular to the surface around the entire perimeter.

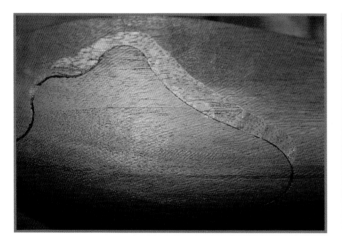

3-5 Remove the wood near the set in perimeter using a flatter gouge, such as a #2 or #3. A #5 may be needed in some of the tighter curves.

3-6 The shell raised above the background of the knee. The background not completely smoothed yet.

3-7 Smooth the background around the shell. Start out with a #49 rasp and finish up with files, riffles, scrapers and sandpaper. The goal is to blend the background so that it is smooth and uniform. The background is now sufficiently blended.

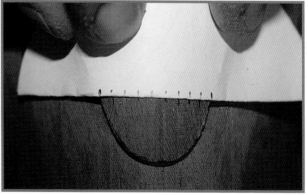

3-8 Find a place on the root that can be evenly divided into nine equal parts and mark the divisions. First mark a piece of paper with the proper divisions and slide the paper up or down the root until the outer two line up with the raised portion.

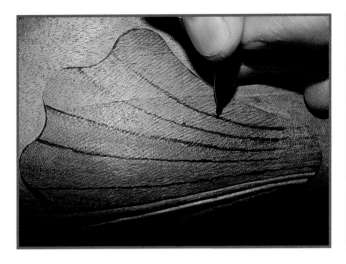

3-9 Sketch in the ray lines connecting the endpoints and the root tick marks.

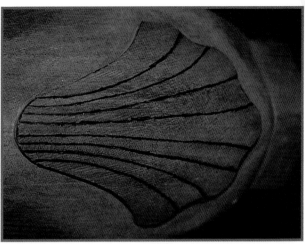

3-10 Extend the ray lines to the bottom of the raised portion. The extensions more or less come straight down. At this point, detailing the lobes is the same as for the applied shell.

3-11 Two of the convex lobes are complete and the concave one is ready for scooping.

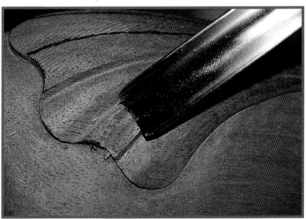

3-12 Use a #9, 13mm gouge to scoop the concave lobe. Be mindful of the grain and careful at the edge to avoid tear out.

3-13 Note how the concave lobe changes to a convex shape at the root. This is because the lobe is too narrow to make it concave.

3-14 A completed shell on a Queen Anne Lowboy.

3-15 A completed shell on a Queen Anne Desk.

the lobe separation points at the outer perimeter. Since there are nine lobes, find a point on the root where the distance across divides evenly into nine parts. Because the shell is curved it is harder to use a rigid ruler to mark the divisions. One technique that will work is to mark out nine equal divisions on a piece of paper. For this shell ⅛ inch should work. So, 10 marks ⅛ inch apart. Now slide the paper up or down the shell root until the two end marks line up with the perimeter of the shell and transfer the marks to the blank. With a pencil make a tick mark on the root at each of the divisions. Figure 3-8 shows the technique and the marks. Now, draw lines connecting a mark on the

root with its corresponding mark at the perimeter. I do this freehand because it is difficult to uniformly conform a template to the curved surface. With a pencil and the heel of your hand as a pivot, sketch in the connecting curves. Figure 3-9 shows this technique. Extend the lines to the bottom of the root so they are evenly distributed across the width. Bringing them straight down should accomplish this. Figure 3-10 shows the lines from top to bottom.

The shell is now ready to be carved. The techniques for carving the shell from this stage forward are identical to those described in the chapter on the applied shell. Refer to that chapter for step by step instructions

on shaping and detailing the lobes. Figures 3-11 through 3-13 show intermediate steps to completing two convex lobes and one concave lobe. Figures 3-14 and 3-15 show a finished shell on a piece of furniture.

Carved foliage on the leg of a chair, or case piece, is an embellishment that is very common and is one sure way of elevating the piece above its peers. Many of the most valued and admired pieces from the 18th century had carved elements on their legs as well as other ornamentation. It is neither necessary nor sufficient that a great piece of furniture be adorned with carved elements. However, many times it's the case that the great pieces have them and in fact, it is the carved elements that elevate the piece in stature. This chapter will describe how to carve one example of foliage on a knee. This type of carving will take a good piece to a higher level. The facing page shows some examples of chair legs with carved foliage.

Carving an embellishment, such as foliage or acanthus, on the knee of a furniture leg is usually the last thing to be done. In this case, that means starting with a fully shaped and smoothed cabriole leg. More often than not, a leg that is going to be carved will be terminated with a ball and claw foot, as is the case here. To begin, locate and mark the centerline of the cabriole leg. One technique for locating the center-line on the knee is to take a narrow piece of paper and fold it around the knee so that it overlaps the back two edges. With the paper taut around the front of the knee, crease it at the back on both sides. Remove the paper and fold it half way between the two crease marks just made. This half waypoint will mark the center of the point where the measurement

was taken. Hold the paper in the original position around the knee and transfer the folded center mark to the leg. Figure 4-1 shows the centerline drawn on the leg.

Now make a carving template from the pattern shown in Figure 4-2. I make many of my templates from boxboard, which is a cereal box, although Mylar is also good choice. I have had good luck with boxboard and it is plentiful and inexpensive. Depending on the shapes involved, use carving tools to cut out the template because they will make cleaner lines in tight places than can be achieved with a scissors. Note that the template is only half of what will actually be drawn on the leg. Because the template is two-dimensional and rather rigid, it will not mold over the three-dimensional

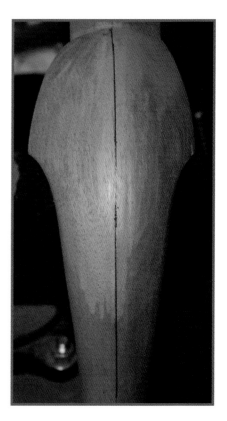

4-1 Draw the centerline far enough down the leg to accommodate the entire template.

31

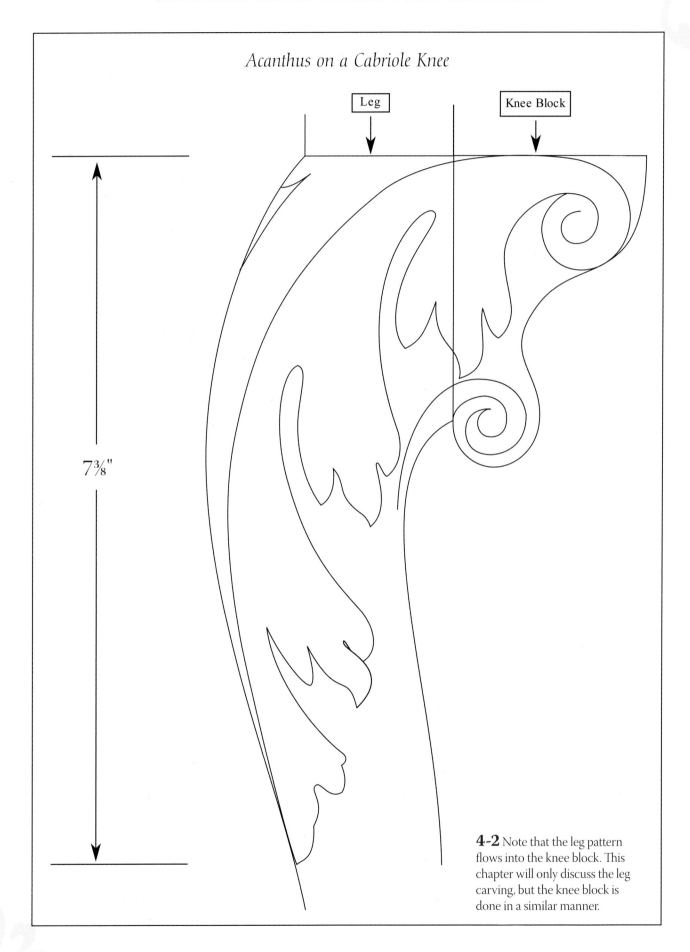

Acanthus on a Cabriole Knee

Leg

Knee Block

7⅜"

4-2 Note that the leg pattern flows into the knee block. This chapter will only discuss the leg carving, but the knee block is done in a similar manner.

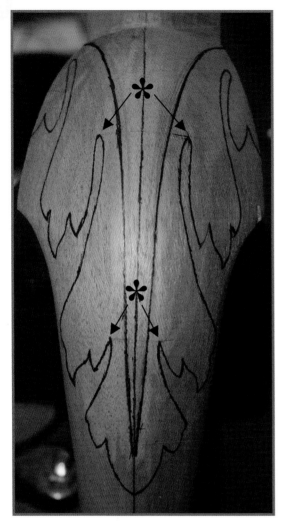

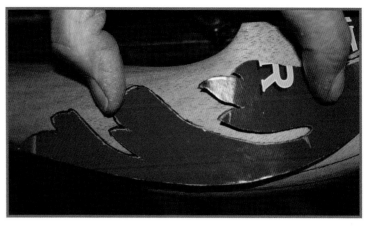

4-4 Trace a small portion of the template and then move it to accommodate the curvature of the leg.

4-3 Set some landmark points, as shown here, to help position the template. The transfer to the leg does not have to be perfect, nor exact, but it should look symmetric and balanced.

4-5 Use a #11, 3mm gouge, to set in along the tight curve.

leg very well without a lot of distortion. One technique for getting around this limitation is to mark specific landmarks on the leg blank and then adjust the position of the template to draw that portion of the template near the landmark and then move to the next one until the entire template is transferred. This technique will probably require a little freehand drawing to blend the partial transfers into one drawing. This technique is not an exact science so if the pattern doesn't go

on as easily as imagined improvise and hit as many of the landmarks as reasonable. The overall effect is more important than the exactness of matching the drawing. Figure 4-3 shows the landmarks. Draw one half of the pattern and then flip the template over and repeat the process on the other half of the leg's centerline. Figure 4-4 shows how the template matches what is drawn on the leg. Figure 4-3 shows the entire pattern drawn on the knee. The goal here is to make the carved area symmetric

about the centerline. This means mirror portions should be at the same height and the same distance from the centerline. It doesn't have to be perfect, just close enough that the eye does not see any asymmetry and it looks good.

The next step is to raise the pattern area by lowering the background around it. In addition, blend the lowered background into the rest of the leg so that the leg surface is smooth and uniform. The techniques are the same as those described in the Shell on Knee chapter with the exception that the perimeter here is more complicated so more and varied gouges will be needed to achieve the shape. Set in around the perimeter matching the local shape of the pattern with a gouge of appropriate sweep and width. My experience is that medium width #3's and #5's work well for blending curves. Medium #7's and #8's are good for tighter curves and volutes. Medium #2's for relatively straight sections and small #11's for tight curves. Figure 4-6 shows the background being blended with a skewed flat chisel and figure 4-7 shows the foliage envelope raised above the background. Note that the background is blended and smoothed with riffler files, scrapers and sandpaper. Pointed riffler files work well to get in the tight spaces close to the carving area.

The next step is to detail the foliage envelope with the individual elements. Note that there is between 1/16 of an inch to 1/8 of an inch depth to the foliage pattern. This is not much depth in which to achieve a 3-D effect. One of the strategies that will be used to help give the illusion of a third dimension is a "rolling hill" contour throughout. That is, the cross-section of the carving at any point should be a continuous up and down, "rolling hill" terrain. Note that this is to be used as a guide and a goal and not to be implemented at all costs in all instances.

The detail elements will be sketched in as the carving proceeds. Since this is a copy of an existing carving it is very helpful, and almost essential, to

4-6 Remove the background material to "raise" the carving envelope. Use flatter gouges to cut into the set in cuts and use files, rifflers, scrapers and sandpaper to blend and smooth the background.

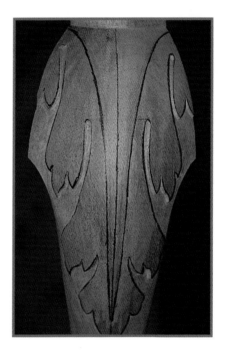

4-7 The foliage envelope has been raised and is ready for layout.

4-8 One angle of the reference model.

have pictures of the original. In this case, the reference model is shown in figures 4-8 through 4-10. First, establish the central "V" portion. Start by sketching lines parallel to the two curved lines. These are labeled "A" as shown in figure 4-11. Separate the central section by carving with a small v-tool on the center line side

of the inner curved line as shown in figure 4-12. Deepen this sufficiently so that there is enough of a ridge to round over as shown in figure 4-13. To reach the desired depth will probably take a couple of iterations with the v-tool and rounding the edge. The idea is to get a smooth and uniform central surface that flows

4-9 Try to visualize how this carving is extracted from the template envelope.

4-10 This shows the bottom of the knee carving on the reference model.

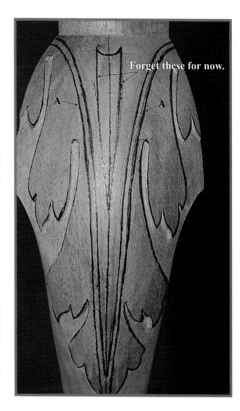

4-11 Sketch the lines labeled "A". These are parallel to the curved lines from the template transfer. Ignore the center layout for now.

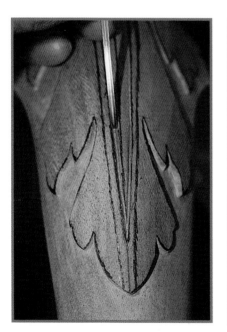

4-12 With a small v-tool start to define the central "V" element.

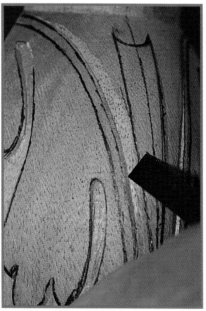

4-13 Round over the ridges of the central "V" with a flat chisel. The goal is to create a smooth surface that flows into the bottom of the "V" tool cut. Make multiple passes to get the desired depth.

4-14 The central "V" area is complete for now.

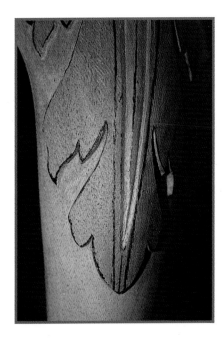

4-15 Note how the depth of the "V" blends back into the higher surface at the bottom.

4-16 Sketch the lines labeled A1 and A2. Study the reference photos to see that these lines will be the centerlines of the outside leaves of this upper cluster. Note also that they will be low.

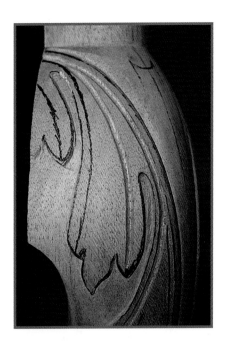

4-17 Use a #11, 2mm gouge, to cut along the lines A1 and A2. Round over the cone with a flat chisel. Deepen and round further as needed.

4-18 Use a series of #9 gouges to scoop out the outer leaves. Use wider ones at first to establish the leaf edge. Deepen the center with a narrower one. Note also the central portion left between the outer two.

into the base of the "V" cut. Figures 4-14 and 4-15 show the desired shape.

The next step will be to outline a couple of leaf clusters. Sketch in the lines labeled A1, A2, B1 and B2 as shown in figure 4-16. Look at the reference pictures and note that A1 and A2 are the low spots that are the centerlines of two different leaves and that A2, also defines the outside edge of the cone element connecting the upper and lower leaf clusters. B1 is also a low spot and defines the inside edge of the cone element. B2 is the low spot and the center for the inside leaf of the lower cluster. Note also that B1 and B2 flow together moving up the leg, as do A1 and A2. In addition, all four of them meet as they converge near the upper part of the leg. Another way to look at this is that all of these lines start from a single point and then flow in different directions depending on their purpose. It is this convergence, and divergence, that gives the appearance that this is a group of leaves that emanate from a common root.

Begin defining the leaf clusters by carving down the A and B lines with a #11, 2mm gouge. Figure 4-17 shows some of these cuts. Round over the edges of the cone using a flat chisel. Figure 4-18 shows more progress on the cone and some definition in the adjacent leaves. Scooping out the center with a #9 gouge of appropriate width further refines each leaf. Use the widest gouge that is not too big because this will give a nice uniform trough that is not too deep. If too narrow of a gouge is used the walls of the leaf will rise

4-19 Divide the central portion into to two more leaves. Use a #9, 5mm gouge, to scoop the center. Note how the scoop cuts taper towards the top of the knee.

4-20 The upper cluster is now shaped.

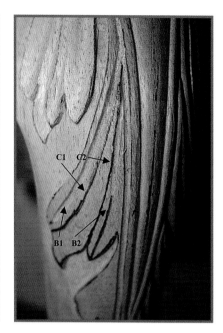

4-21 Draw and carve the lines B1 and B2. These are analogous to the lines A1 and A2 in the upper cluster. C1 and C2 will remain high and indicate the edge of the leaves. There are only three leaves it the lower cluster.

4-22 Scoop the individual leaves with some #9 gouges.

too steeply and they will be thin and fragile. In addition, they will not look good. For the operation I used 13mm, 10mm, 7 mm and 5mm gouges, depending on the width of the leaf and the depth desired. In general, start out with a wider gouge to establish the edges and switch to narrower ones to deepen the central trough. I like deeper carvings because they will cast darker shadows, which will translate into a bolder and more dramatic look.

Also, in figure 4-18 note that another line has been drawn. This will divide the center portion of this cluster into two more leaves. Use a #9, 5mm gouge to define the leaves as shown in figure 4-19. Note that the center of the leaf is deeper at the tip and shallower as it flows up the stem. Figure 4-20 shows the upper cluster defined and separated into four leaves. At the end, a few highlight lines will be added, but the shaping is now done.

The lower leaf cluster will be shaped in the same manner as the upper one. Figure 4-21 shows the layout lines and some early carving. The lines B1 and B2 are the centerlines of the leaves on the inner and outer edges of the cluster and will be low. The lines C1 and C2 will remain high and will define the middle leaf between the outer two. This cluster only has three leaves in it. In a similar manner as before, scoop out the outer leaves with a series of # 9 gouges as shown in figure 4-22. Now, scoop the center leaf. Clean up the surfaces using scrapers and rifflers as needed. The goal is to get smooth and blended surfaces by removing the facets left by the gouges. Sometimes it is easier to achieve this final surface with a scraper than a carving tool. Figure 4-23 shows a

4-23 Clean up the surface with scrapers. The goal is to get smooth surfaces that flow into each other.

4-24 The completed lower cluster.

4-25 Each of these layout lines will remain high. Note the area labeled "X." A leaf tip is extracted and separated using a #7, 4mm gouge.

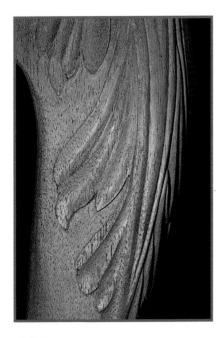

4-26 Each of the individual leaves are shaped using a series of #9 gouges. Use similar techniques as before.

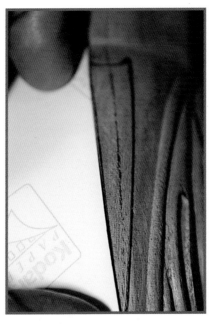

4-27 Draw the triangle detail in the upper center portion of the knee. Use a flexible straight edge to draw a straight line on the highly curved surface.

scraper cleaning up one of the leaf surfaces. Figure 4-24 shows the completed lower cluster.

There is one more small section below the lower leaf cluster. Figure 4-25 shows the layout lines. These lines will remain high and be the divisions between the leaves. Using the #9 gouges scoop between the lines to shape the leaves. Figure 4-26 shows the results.

It is now time to add the scooped out central detail on the upper portion of the knee as shown in figure 4-8 of the reference model. The semi-circular upper termination is approximately ½ of an inch down from the top of the knee. Draw in the triangle as shown in figure 4-27. It is a little tricky to draw straight lines on such a curved surface so I used the side of a photograph as a flexible straight edge. It's not perfect, but it works okay. Figure

4-28 Here is the layout for the triangle detail. Set in along the semi-circular arc with a #8, 10 mm gouge. Hold the chisel so that the handle is parallel to the post. This will be at an angle that will not under cut the arc. Scoop out the inner portion with a series of #9 gouges. Strive for straight lines and smooth curves.

4-29 The triangle detail complete.

4-30 There are three pair of semi-circular cuts along the length of the each cone. The placement is not critical, so place them by eye, based on the reference model.

4-31 Use a #7, 4mm gouge, to set in perpendicular to the surface. Be careful not to undercut because this will weaken the arc.

4-28 shows the triangle layout. When the triangle is drawn, set in along the semi-circular arc with a #8, 10mm gouge. It is important not to under cut this portion or the arc is very likely to chip off. The correct position of the gouge is to have the handle parallel to the post of the leg. The set in cut should be very close to vertical. This will provide enough support material so the arc will not break. Use #9 gouges to scoop out the triangle into the semi-circular set in cut. Figure 4-29 shows the completed triangle.

All of the shaping is now done. Only a few details remain. In the reference model, there are three pairs of small semi-circular ticks in each of the cones. Figure 4-30 shows the layout for these marks on one of the cones. The members of each pair are close together and the pairs are separated. Lay these out by eye. These are delicate cuts so take care and don't press too hard with the gouge. In addition, make sure not to under cut the stop cut or the semi-circular portion will break. With a #7, 4mm gouge, positioned as shown in figure 4-31 make a stop cut along the centerline of the cone. Position the gouge so the arc is symmetric with, and perpendicular to, the centerline of the cone. In theory, the stop cut should be 90° to the surface of the wood. To insure against an undercut, try to cut a little greater than 90°. If it is too much, trim it back. Now with the concave portion of the gouge facing up make a small cut into the stop cut. Figure 4-32 shows the result. To make the second member of the pair, move slightly up the cone and make another stop cut and cut back into it as before. Now repeat this on the other two pairs. Note that as the cone narrows, the stop cuts are neither as wide nor as deep. And the last pair near the tip is smaller still. These small details add a lot to the overall effect of casting shadows and making the carving seem alive. Figure 4-33 shows the two pair on one of the cones. Repeat the process on the other cone.

The last details to add will be some accent lines in each of the leaves. I use a narrow #11 for this. Either a 0.5mm, or a 1mm, gouge works well. Typically, there will be a longer line down the center and a couple of shorter ones on either side of center near the tip. Figure 4-34 shows a typical example. When these are done the carving is complete. Figure 4-35 shows the completed knee.

Because this leg is destined for a chair, the carving on the knee block is a continuation of what was just carved on the knee. For that reason the elements near the leg edges were not carved now. They will be carved as one surface with the knee blocks after the leg is installed on the chair and the knee blocks are attached.

4-32 With the #7, 4mm gouge, concave side up, cut into the stop cut made in the previous step. Move up the cone slightly and cut the second member of the pair. Note the first pair behind the chisel.

4-33 The two pair of cuts are now complete.

4-34 Use a #11, 0.5mm (½ mm), or a 1mm gouge, to make accent cuts in each leaf. Put a longer one down the middle and shorter ones on either side of the center near the tip of the leaf.

4-35 The knee carving is now complete and the leg is ready to be installed in the chair.

Chapter 5
Applied Philadelphia Shell

This applied shell is one of the simpler motifs to visualize and to carve. However, it is very elegant and significantly enhances the piece to which it is applied. This style of shell would typically be placed on the front rail of a chair, the long rails of a footstool or the lower face frame member of a dressing table (lowboy) or a chest on frame (highboy). Most shells of this type are geometrically similar, although they come in various sizes. The shell that I am going to present here is from a chair, but I have scaled this same design to fit on a footstool. The following page shows a couple of examples of furniture with an applied shell.

Before one can begin carving this shell two patterns are required. One is the front facing profile and the other is the side profile. Figures 5-1 and 5-2 show the patterns that I will use for this discussion. Note that this pattern can easily be scaled to meet the needs of the specific application.

Transfer the front profile to the wood blank as shown in figure 5-3. Don't transfer the ray lines because they are not needed at this point and they would just be erased during shaping. However, do make little tick marks on the edge where the ray lines terminate. These will be used in a later operation. In all applications that I have encountered, the grain of the wood is running horizontally when the shell is viewed from the front. Now, cut along the front profile line using a bandsaw

or a scroll saw. Next, remove the saw marks along the perimeter using a file as shown in figure 5-4. This does not have to be perfect because much of the perimeter will be removed in the shaping and carving steps. However, make sure that the bottom part of the edge is acceptable because this is the portion that will remain. It will be difficult to file this after the carving is done.

There is just a little more preparation needed before shaping begins. Start by drawing a line around the perimeter ⅛ of an inch up from the bottom. This can be done by eye using a pencil and your finger as a guide. (Figure 5-5) Next, mark the high spot on top of the blank as shown in figure 5-6. This area is the only part that will not be touched during the shaping operation. Now

fix the shell blank to a larger piece of scrap wood using double stick tape. The shell needs to be held firmly for shaping and carving and I find it easier to tape it to a scrap piece and then clamp the scrap piece to the bench. I use carpet tape for this operation and it holds amazingly well. Sometimes it can hold too well so take care when removing the completed shell from the scrap. Figure 5-7 shows how little tape needs to be applied. To get a good seal between the shell blank and the scrap piece do the following: With the tape applied, press the shell to the scrap and then clamp them in a vice. The shell blank is now sufficiently secured for the duration of the process.

Now it is time to shape the profiled blank. With the shell and scrap piece

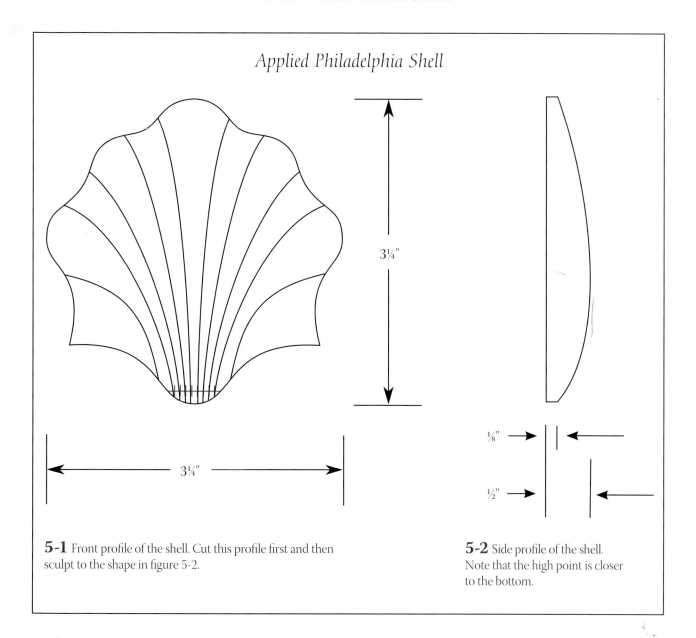

Applied Philadelphia Shell

3¼"

3¼"

⅛"

½"

5-1 Front profile of the shell. Cut this profile first and then sculpt to the shape in figure 5-2.

5-2 Side profile of the shell. Note that the high point is closer to the bottom.

fixed to the bench, rasp down to the ⅛ inch perimeter line. Start aggressively near the edge and lighten up as you get closer to the central high spot. I use a Nicholson, #49, patternmakers rasp for this operation. The #49 is an aggressive cut, so it removes wood quickly. I like this tool better than a bastard cut rasp because of the random tooth pattern. The bastard cut will tend to make the same grooves deeper, whereas the #49 will not

concentrate in one spot and removes wood more evenly.

The goal in this step is to have a smooth, continuous surface that is high in the central area and falling off in all directions down to the ⅛ inch line at the edge. Figure 5-8 shows this shaping step almost complete. Stop a little shy of the perimeter line and then switch to a bastard cut file. This is a smoother cut than the #49 and it will be used to clean up the surface and take it

down to the edge line. Figure 5-9 shows progress after the filing operation. Now a few layout lines are needed before starting the carving operations.

Transfer the ray lines from the front shell profile drawing onto the sculpted shell blank. This is going to require some freehand drawing because of the curved surface. Because this shell has nine lobes, five convex, and four concave, there will be ten lines that define them. Two

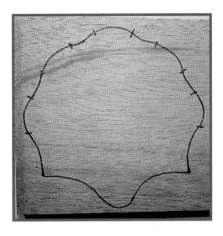

5-3 The front profile is transferred to the wooden blank. Note the tick marks along the upper edge. These will be transferred to the edge after the profile is cut.

5-4 File the edges of the blank before carving.

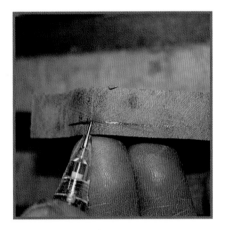

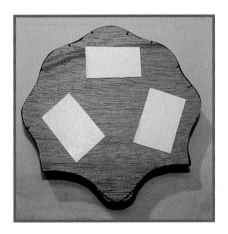

5-5 Using your finger as a guide, draw a line around the perimeter ⅛ inch up from the bottom.

5-6 The mark shows the high spot on the shell. The shell falls off in all directions from this point.

5-7 Use double stick tape to fix the shell blank to a piece of scrap. Note the small amount of tape. If too much tape is used it may be difficult to separate the carved shell from the scrap.

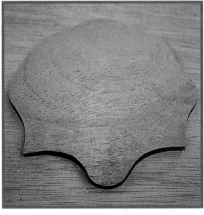

5-8 This is as much as can be done with the rasp. Now switch to a file.

5-9 The blank is now filed smooth and ready to be carved.

5-10 Using the heel of your hand as a pivot, sketch in one of the outside lines.

5-11 Both of the outside lines are drawn on the blank.

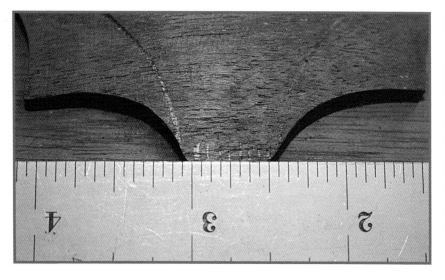

5-12 Find a place near the bottom where the distance between the two outside lines is nine units apart.

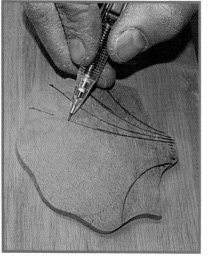

5-13 Again, use the heel of your hand as a pivot, and connect the marks as shown here.

will define the outside edge and the other eight will separate the lobes. With a pencil and the heel of your hand as a pivot, sketch in the two outside lines. Figures 5-10 and 5-11 show how this is done and what it should look like upon completion.

Now sketch in the eight interior lines. The ends of each ray line are marked on the edge surface. This was done in the beginning when the face profile was drawn. The tricky part now is to have each of these

lines flow nicely and evenly between the two outside lines. To achieve this, find a portion near the root end of the shell that is evenly divisible into nine segments. Use a ruler with gradations of at least $\frac{1}{16}$ths, or possibly finer. Slide the ruler up or down the root end of the shell until you find a place where the distance between the two outside ray lines is exactly nine units apart. Make a small pencil mark at each of the intermediate eight segments

as shown in figure 5-12. With the heel of your hand as a pivot, connect each of these tick marks to the corresponding one along the outer edge. See figure 5-3 for the outer edge marks. Figure 5-13 shows the technique. The shaped blank is now ready for detail carving.

As with all carving it is best to know what you are trying to achieve before you start. Figure 5-14 shows the result that will be achieved from the next series of steps. Start by cutting straight down along the outside lines. A #5, 12mm gouge, should match this curve nicely. If the gouge doesn't match the line exactly let the tool "redraw" the line as the cut is made. The idea is to have a nice smooth curve. After the initial "stop" cut use the same gouge, or a slightly flatter one, to remove the wood from the edge terminating into the cut just made. Now repeat the process of deepening the stop cut and removing wood. The final depth will go to within $\frac{1}{16}$" of the bottom. Figure 5-15 shows more progress. Figure 5-16 shows the completed operation. Repeat the same series of cuts on the other side.

The next series of steps will define and shape the lobes of the shell. A few words of caution are warranted here, and they need to be kept in mind during the entire process. Because many of the cuts that are going to be made are in extremely short grained areas, take care to avoid, or minimize chip out. When chip out occurs, and it will, glue the piece back and continue. Cyano-acrylate glue used with the aerosol activator works great for reattaching chipped off parts. The thin version of the glue works well because it will quickly wick into small cracks. Apply the glue and spray with the activator. The glue sets instantly so work can continue. Sometimes if the chipped piece is small enough or depending where it is, the area can be reshaped with no visible harm. This is a judgement call that has to be made depending on the situation.

5-14 This shows what the next series of steps will achieve.

5-15 Use a #5, 12mm gouge, to make a stop cut along one of the outer lines. Remove the wood from the outside edge up to this stop cut. Remove the material with a flatter gouge.

5-16 One of the corners has been removed.

46

Start with the ray lines that were drawn earlier. These ray lines are separation lines between adjacent lobes. The strategy is to cut straight down along these lines. Round away from them for a convex lobe, and bevel into them for a concave one. When this stage is complete the convex lobes will be shaped and the concave ones will be defined and ready for detailing.

With a shallow gouge, say a #2 or #3, 8mm, gently cut straight down along one of the ray lines. You can use a mallet or hand pressure, but in either case be gentle and make the cut shallow. It is best to start somewhere in the middle and then move to the edges. The middle cuts are less susceptible to chip out and will let you get a sense of what the cuts feel like. The most vulnerable place for these cuts is the root of the shell where the remaining wood is very narrow and across the grain. In these areas I would use just the corner of the gouge and drag it in a slicing motion rather than stamping down on it. In addition, make a shallow cut, then relieve it on both sides and repeat the process. This grain is so fragile that the pressure from the bevel of the chisel as the cut is made can be enough to break off a piece. I know people who use an Exacto knife for this. This would work all right, but I am more comfortable with the carving tool. Figure 5-17 shows early progress defining these separation lines. The separation lines will get deeper as they fan away from the root. When they reach the edge of the shell they will be almost

5-17 Cut straight down along the separation lines and bevel into it from the concave side and round over on the convex side

5-18 Strive to make the ridge lines, and "V", as shown here. This will strengthen the ridge and help to prevent chip out.

down to the bottom. Keep them a little bit away from the bottom to prevent breaking through, but the deeper they go the more dramatic the shadows will be.

The remainder of defining the lobes is a repetition of these steps. That is, deepen the separation line and then round over or bevel the adjacent

portion. Another caution area is the center most lobes at the perimeter. The separation cuts are ninety degrees to the grain at this point and the center lobe can easily break away. If a v-tool is used in this area, the chance of breakout is very high. However, by carefully scoring the wood across the grain and relieving

5-19 The convex lobes are rounded, and the concave ones are ready to be carved.

5-20 To hollow out the concave lobe use the widest #9 gouge that will fit the width. Early progress is shown here.

back into this cut, tear out can be greatly minimized and in most cases eliminated.

Other vulnerable areas are the ridge lines on either side of the concave lobes. My experience is that it is easy to make the angled walls that support the concave center too steep when beveling into the separation cuts. This will make for a very sharp, narrow, and fragile ridge line. Take care to make this a shallower angle. This will provide more material below the ridge line, which will translate into a much stronger and significantly less fragile area. Figure 5-18 shows a good angle to strive for.

With all of these things in mind continue with the same techniques until all of the ridge lines are fully established, the convex lobes are rounded and the concave ones are ready to be scooped. Figure 5-19 shows how this should look.

Finally, with a #9, 10mm or 13mm gouge, start to scoop out the flat portions between two adjacent ridge lines. Figure 5-20 shows the beginning of this process. Start a little before the end and work towards the edge. The goal is to get a nice, smooth and even curve between the ridge lines. Because the ridge lines converge, use a narrower gouge as the cut moves towards the root. Note that the concave cuts will get shallower as they get narrower and eventually they will feather to no depth. Theoretically, I think that there would be a slight concave shape along the entire length of a lobe. However, as a practical matter the concave shape will stop somewhere near the high point of the root. This is because the lobes are so narrow at that point that it is impractical to continue. Thus, in this area round over the remaining portions of the concave lobes. Figure 5-21 shows how this area should look.

The shell is now substantially complete. The last step is to put a few detail lines in the wings. I use a #11, 0.5mm gouge, for this. Because the grain gets quite short when making these cuts, take care not to chip out a piece. Be mindful of the grain and change direction if needed. Figure 5-22 shows the completed shell.

5-21 Because the lobes are very narrow towards the bottom of the shell round over the concave ones also.

5-22 Add a few detail lines on the outer wings and the shell is complete.

Chapter 6
Philadelphia Rosette

This chapter will describe how to carve an applied rosette that would be used to terminate a large swan neck molding that is at the top of a high chest of drawers or a tall case clock. Specifically, the subject of this chapter was originally from a Philadelphia high chest of drawers. The image below shows my version of this rosette. Although there are many variations of applied rosettes, they all start out as a turned blank that is then carved. The turned profile for this one is shown in figure 6-1.

To understand the elements in this rosette, think about them in a couple of different ways concurrently. Look at the completed version in figure 6-2 and concentrate on the lower tier. This tier is one major element repeated six times around the perimeter. This is the outer ring of the 60° segment in figure 6-1. Now concentrate on the second tier, which is layered on top of the first. This is actually a smaller version of tier one that is rotated 60°. This is the middle ring of the 60° segment in figure 6-1. Finally, concentrate on the

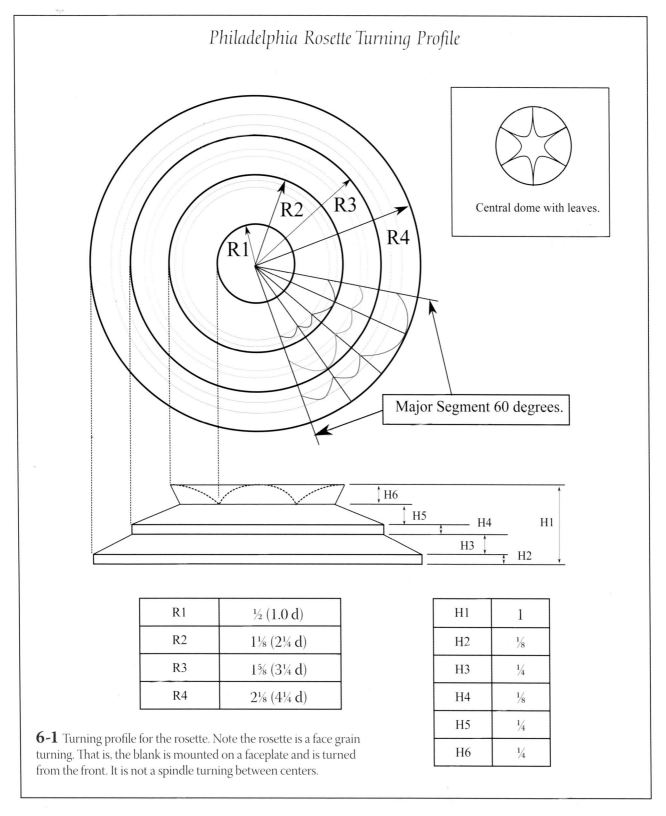

Philadelphia Rosette Turning Profile

Central dome with leaves.

Major Segment 60 degrees.

R1	½ (1.0 d)
R2	1⅛ (2¼ d)
R3	1⅝ (3¼ d)
R4	2⅛ (4¼ d)

H1	1
H2	⅛
H3	¼
H4	⅛
H5	¼
H6	¼

6-1 Turning profile for the rosette. Note the rosette is a face grain turning. That is, the blank is mounted on a faceplate and is turned from the front. It is not a spindle turning between centers.

top tier. This is yet a smaller version of tiers one and two that is rotated back 60° from tier two and in the same orientation as tier one. This is the inner ring of the 60° segment in figure 6-1. Another way to think about how it is constructed is to look at one 60° pie slice that includes all three tiers. See 60° segment in figure 6-1. The rosette is comprised of six of these slices repeated around the perimeter. With this in mind, it is time to draw some layout lines.

6-2 Study the completed rosette to help understand what are the repeated segments and how they relate to each other.

Because the rosette is one item repeated six times around the perimeter, divide the blank into six equal parts. A good way to do this is to use the layout template in figure 6-3. First place a pencil dot at the center of the blank. Now, center the blank on the template and transfer all of the diameters to the blank. The easiest way to do this is by eye. Use both ends of a diameter on the template and the center of the blank and sight a straight line between them. Draw this line on the blank. Figure 6-4 shows the technique. Also, draw two concentric circles on each tier as shown in the figure 6-5. These circles are illustrated in figure 6-1. They will be used as depth guides when forming the petals. The major

lines are going to separate the six repeatable segments and the minor lines are the centerlines of these segments. The remaining lines are half way between the major and minor lines. The blank now has sixteen radial lines that are 15° apart. Figure 6-6 shows the blank divided into 15° wedges with guide circles on each tier. The layout is now complete.

Fix the blank to a larger backer board with double stick tape. The backer board will be used to hold the rosette blank in place while carving. The carving progression will be to round the perimeter of each 30° wedge to a circular arc on each of the three layers. Start with a v-tool and cut straight down at

the edge of one of the radial lines. Start near the perimeter and work the depth into the next circle. Figure 6-7 shows the technique, figure 6-8 shows intermediate progress, and figure 6-9 shows the result. Round over the corners formed by the "V" to the next radial line in each direction. Use a #7, 16mm gouge, for the outer layer and a #7, 10mm one for the middle and inner layers. Figure 6-10 shows an example on each layer. Note that when cleaning away the waste between the segments, you want to retain the angle of the surface below. Repeat this process around the perimeter of each of the three layers. Figure 6-11 shows all three layers with rounded, 30° wedge segments.

Select one of the 30° segments on the outer perimeter. This wedge is going to be separated into two equal petals. The detailed segment shown in figure 6-1 shows the idea. Separate this 30° wedge into two 15° ones using the same techniques as earlier. That is, use the v-tool to cut straight down on the centerline, and incrementally work to the depth of the second circle. Round the "V" corners with a #7, 10mm gouge, using the same techniques as before. Note that the inside arc of the 15° petal goes a little deeper than the outside ones. Figure 6-12 shows one of the 30° wedges separated into two 15° petals.

Move to one of the adjacent 30° wedges and up to the second layer. Separate the 30° wedge on this layer into two 15° petals in the same manner as on the outer layer. Figure

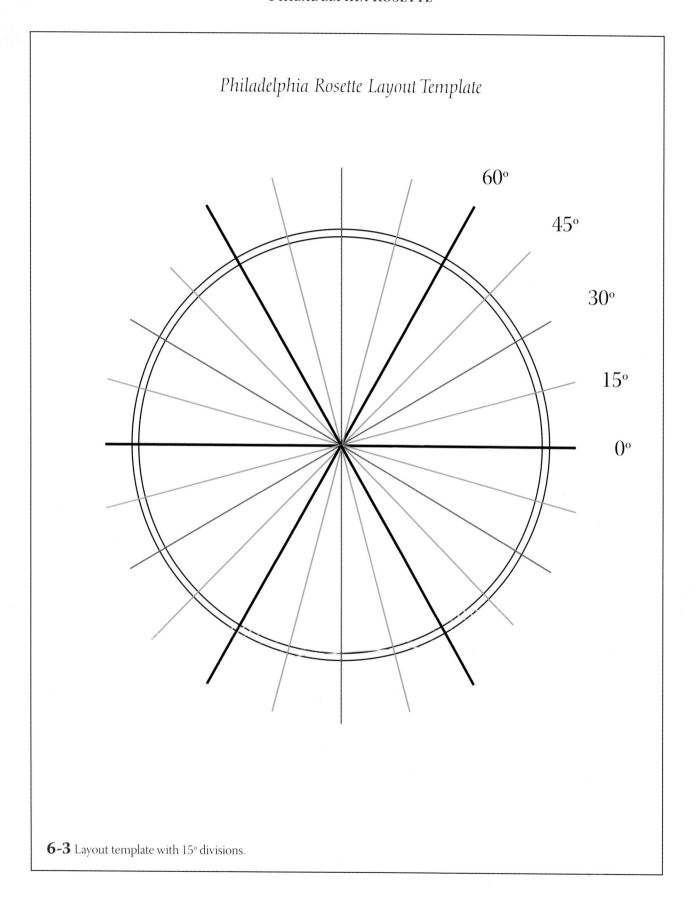

Philadelphia Rosette Layout Template

60°

45°

30°

15°

0°

6-3 Layout template with 15° divisions.

6-4 Use the layout template to sight and draw the diameter lines 15° apart.

6-5 Use a compass to draw guide circles on each tier.

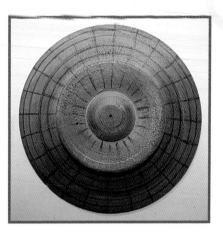

6-6 Blank layout is complete.

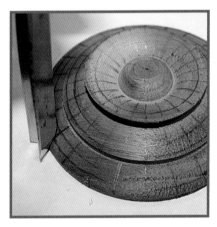

6-7 Iteratively, use a v-tool to cut straight down on one of the radial lines.

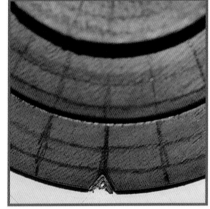
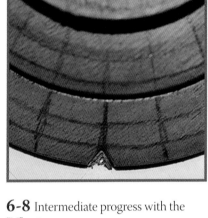

6-8 Intermediate progress with the "V" cuts.

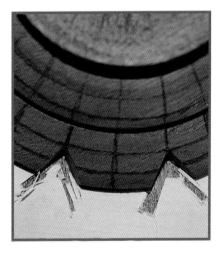

6-9 The "V" cuts are complete for the first lower segment.

6-1 shows the idea and figure 6-13 shows the result.

Now move back to the original 30° wedge and go to the third layer. In the same manner separate this wedge into two smaller ones. The technique is the same as before. Again figure 6-1 shows the intent and figure 6-14 shows the result.

The last three operations taken together have defined one of the six repeatable segments. Cut the remaining five around the perimeter.

The next series of operations will contour each petal and further separate them from each other. The

separation between petals will be ridge lines formed by carving a concave surface on each petal. The ridge is the intersection of two adjacent concave surfaces. A #7 gouge will give a nice concave surface. Start on one of the large petals on the outer layer and with #7, 20mm gouge, begin to cut between the lines. Take care to stay inside the radial lines because these will become the ridges. As the cut moves inward radially, continue the concave surface up to the base of the two small petals on layer two. This means that the depth of the smaller petals on layer two will increase to drop down as the concave surface on layer one deepens. This is one of those cases that is easy to describe and visualize, but more difficult to execute. It will not be completely straightforward to run the concave surface simply into the next layer because of the constraints due to the tool size, the petals on the second layer and the grain direction. Use smaller gouges as needed and any other tool that might be useful. Sometimes a small skew chisel works well in a tight spot like the area between the two small

6-10 The rounded corner of the "V" cuts on each layer in a 30° segment.

6-11 The first round over refinement is now complete on all three tiers.

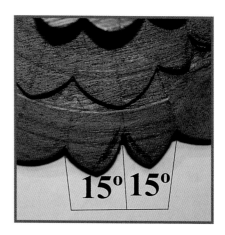

6-12 Separate one 30° wedge into two 15° wedges using the same techniques of first cutting a "V" and rounding the corners.

6-13 Move up to the second tier and one 30° wedge to the left. In the same manner separate this 30° wedge into two 15° ones and round the corners.

6-14 Move up to the third tier and back to the 30° wedge that was used in tier one. Separate this wedge into two 15° ones in the same manner as previously noted. Note that this is one of the 60° wedges illustrated in figure 1.

6-15 Early progress on the rosette.

6-16 The first 30° concave surface on tier one is complete. Now repeat this operation on the remaining five 30° petals on tier one.

6-17 On layer one, scoop each of the smaller petals with a ridge between them.

6-18 Detail of a large and two smaller petals on tier two. Note that the smaller petals are one concave surface instead of two as on tier one.

6-19 Tier three is done in the same manner as tier two. That is, the two small petal wedges are shaped as one concave surface. Here one segment is complete.

6-20 One segment on all three layers is complete.

6-21 Outline the petals of the central dome using a #7, 4mm gouge.

6-22 Remove the material between the petals on the dome.

6-23 Separate the dome petals with a narrow #11 gouge. Stipple the center of the dome.

6-24 Add detail lines to all petals as shown. Vary the length with the center ones being the longest.

6-25 The goal is to make the front and back surfaces meet at a thin line at the perimeter. This will give a nice crisp outline to the completed rosette. Early progress on relieving the back. Use a narrow, #11, 1mm gouge, along the radial lines between adjacent petals.

petals on the second layer. Figure 6-15 shows early progress and figure 6-16 shows one of the large outer petals complete. Repeat this process for the remaining five large petals on the outer layer.

Now move to the smaller petals on layer one and repeat the process using smaller gouges since the petals are smaller. The concept is the same as are the execution techniques. Figure 6-17 shows this operation completed.

The petals on layer two will be shaped in a very similar manner with the exception that there will not be a ridge between the two smaller petals. The two-petal wedge will be contoured with one concave surface instead of two. Figure 6-18 shows one small petal and one large petal wedge complete. Repeat the sequence around the perimeter of the second layer.

Layer three is treated the same as layer two. That is, the small petal segment has one concave surface.

Because the wedges on layer three are narrower, a #7 will not be deep enough to give a nice bold curve, so switch to a #8 or #9. The techniques are the same as before. Figure 6-19 shows one single and one double petal on layer three. Because the smaller petal wedges on this layer are especially narrow, cut between them with a #11, 1mm gouge. Repeat this on the remainder of layer three. Figure 6-20 shows one segment on all three layers complete to this point.

57

6-26 Intermediate progress relieving the back. Notice how the perimeter is collapsing to a line.

6-27 The relieved back on one segment.

6-28 The completed rosette.

6-29 The reason for carving the back in this way is so that the edges of the rosette taper to a thin line. This will generate a crisper visual line when viewed from the front.

The central dome element is next. See figure 6-1 for a drawing of what is intended for the central dome. The area in the top center of the dome is lowered with the tips of the six leaves meeting near the top. Use a #7, 4mm gouge, to set in around the tips of the leaves. Figure 6-21 shows these outline cuts. Remove the material in the top center of the dome between the tips. Figure 6-22 shows this step. Separate the six leaves with a #11, 1mm gouge. Use a stippling tool or a pointed object to dent the central background of the dome. This will simulate the center of a flower. Figure 6-23 shows this detail.

The last step to finishing this rosette carving is to cut some detail shadow lines in each of the leaves and relieve the back around the perimeter. Use a #11, 1 mm, or a 0.5mm gouge to cut two or three lines in each petal. Vary the lines in length as shown in figure 6-24.

Finally relieve the material from the back around the perimeter. Figures 6-25 through 6-27 show the process. This will form a dark shadow between the front of the rosette and its background surface. This will add visual depth. In addition, it will crisp up the perimeter lines giving it a lighter look. Figures 6-28 and 6-29 respectively show the front and the back of a completed rosette.

Chapter 7
Philadelphia Flame Finial

Flame finials adorn the tops of larger case pieces such as tall case clocks, secretaries and high chests. They are embellishments that are striking and above the common place. Flame finials differed by region in style and complexity. Some were more stylized and geometric like the Newport spiral flame or a Boston corkscrew. Others were more organic like those produced in Philadelphia. In most cases, the construction is similar in that the flame and the underlying urn are separate pieces fitted together with a circular mortise and tenon. In addition, there is a circular tenon on the bottom of the urn that will fit into a mortise that will attach it to the case. In both instances, the tenons are not glued. The finial that is described in this chapter is from a Philadelphia high chest of drawers. My version is shown at right.

The urn for this flame is not carved so it will not be discussed here. However, a turning profile for it is provided. To start the flame, begin by turning a blank to the specifications shown in figure 7-1. After the blank is turned, some layout and understanding are needed before carving begins. The layout starts by dividing the blank into six equal longitudinal sections. These do not have to be perfect, so sketch them in by eye. Divide the top into six, 60° sections. First draw a diameter and then divide each half into thirds. Note that there are now three diameter lines on the top. Make a short tick mark on both ends of each diameter down the face of the blank.

Figure 7-2 shows the top divisions and the short tick marks. Hold the blank so that the top is pointing slightly down and away. Sight the extension of one of the tick marks at the top down to the bottom of the curved portion of the flame. This is shown in figure 7-3. Repeat this process on the remaining five tick marks. Holding the blank in a more horizontal position, connect the mark on top with the corresponding one at the base. Figure 7-4 shows the first longitudinal line.

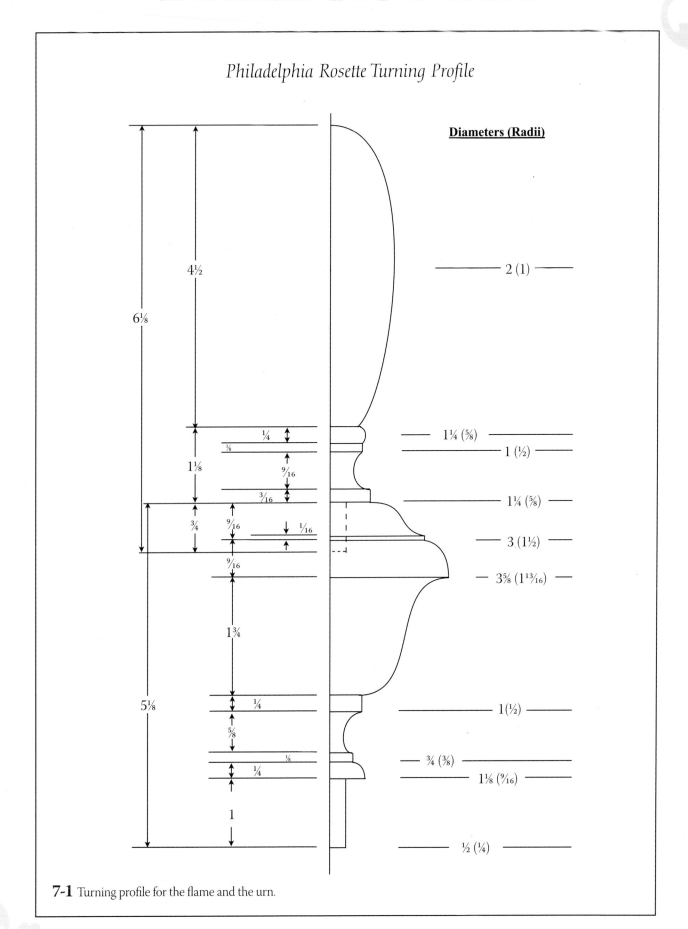

Philadelphia Rosette Turning Profile

Diameters (Radii)

7-1 Turning profile for the flame and the urn.

7-2 Divide the top surface of the flame blank into six 60° sections. First divide it in half and then divide each half into thirds. Also, mark the end of each line on the vertical surface of the flame.

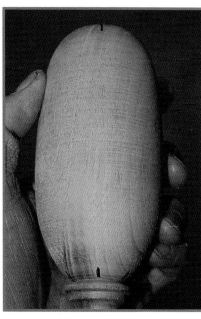

7-3 Hold the blank with the top pointing down slightly. This is a good position to sight a straight line down the length of the flame. Mark the opposite end of the line at the bottom of the blank. Sight this line by eye.

7-4 To draw a longitudinal line, hold the blank as shown. While sighting the line between the two endpoints draw part of the line from both directions. Sketch a longitudinal line.

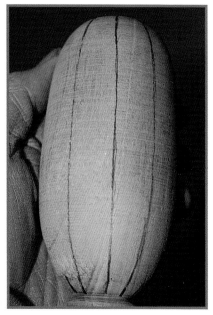

7-5 At both the top and bottom, mark the point half way between adjacent lines of longitude. Mark these in red to help differentiate them from the other lines.

Repeat this on the other five pair of tick marks. Again by eye, make a little tick mark at the top and at the bottom half way between each pair of adjacent lines of longitude. Connect corresponding marks. These are shown in red in figure 7-5. The lines of longitude, and the marks between, are going to be used as a guide to draw s-curves that will represent the ridge and valley lines. These lines will define the various flame components.

Now draw an s-curve from the bottom of one longitudinal line to the top of the longitudinal line that is two segments counter clockwise. Study figure 7-6 to understand where the various layout lines are drawn. To draw this s-curve, hold the blank approximately parallel in one hand with the top pointing away. Pick one of the longitudinal lines. At the bottom of this line, start drawing an s-curve. From the bottom, the curve will start out moving up and to the right with a concave down orientation. Draw about 2 inches up the blank and stop. Figure 7-7 shows the s-curve starting at the bottom. Now turn the blank so that the base is pointing away and slightly up. Rotate the blank so that the s-curve just drawn is visible on the right and that the line of longitude two segments to the left is also visible. Begin drawing another s-curve from the top of the second longitudinal line up and to the right. This curve will have a concave down orientation from this perspective. Draw about 2 inches and stop. Figure 7-8 shows the s-curve starting at the top. Work from

61

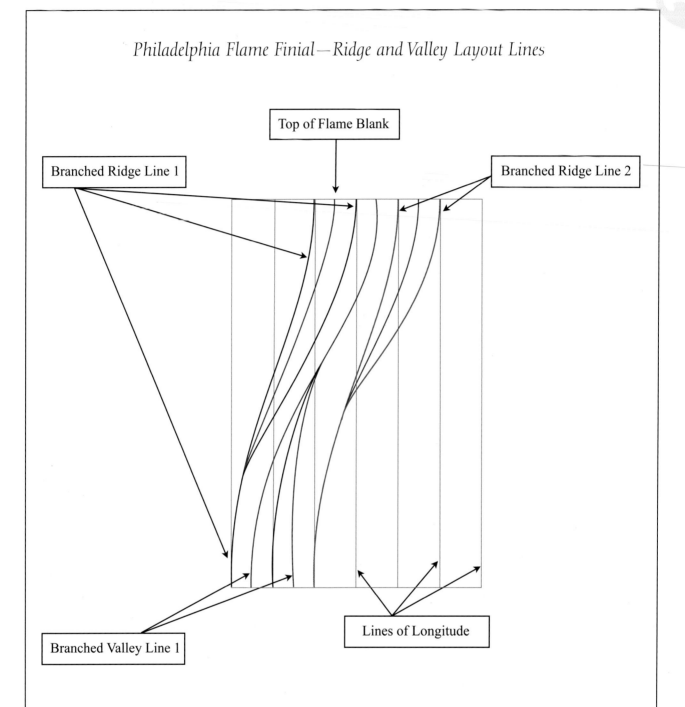

Philadelphia Flame Finial — Ridge and Valley Layout Lines

Top of Flame Blank

Branched Ridge Line 1

Branched Ridge Line 2

Branched Valley Line 1

Lines of Longitude

7-6 Branched ridge and branched valley lines. Although only two sets of the ridge lines and one set of valley lines are shown there are three branched ridge lines and three branched valley lines interlaced and distributed uniformly around the perimeter of the blank. Note that there is a valley line between any two adjacent ridge lines and there is a ridge line between any two adjacent valley lines. This diagram is conceptual and meant to show the relative placement of the ridge and valley lines. Because these lines will be drawn on a three dimensional surface this diagram cannot be transferred directly to that surface.

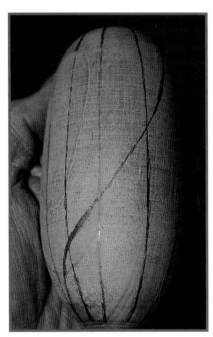

7-7 A portion of the s-curve starting from the bottom.

7-8 A portion of the s-curve starting from the top. Note that the blank is now held in the opposite position from the previous orientation. Also note that the top is moved two lines of longitude to one side.

7-9 One of the s-curves completed.

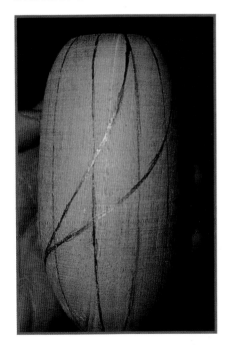

7-10 The line on the left is the first curve drawn. The branch on the right has been added in this step.

both directions and connect the two s-curves with a smooth, gentle continuous curve. Flip and rotate the blank as needed to sight and draw the connecting curve. Figure 7-9 shows the s-curve complete. This s-curve will be one of the ridge lines when the carving is complete. There will be three ridge lines identical to the one just drawn equally spaced around the perimeter of the blank.

This particular flame has a complication that others do not. That is, each ridge line has a branch that starts a bit up from the bottom and spirals around to meet the top of the longitudinal line, three segments counter clockwise. The s-curve at the top of this branch is very similar to the top of the original s-curve. Looking at it another way,

this branch is an s-curve that starts at the bottom of the original line of longitude and spirals around to terminate at the top of the line of longitude three segments counter clockwise. The technique to draw this branch s-curve is the same as the original one. Figure 7-10 shows the branch line complete. Note that the curve from the bottom branches to connect to the longitudinal line farther to the right. It is not critical where the branch occurs, but it is better if it comes in the lower third of the blank. This branched ridge-line will be repeated two more times around the surface of the blank. Now label these curves as shown in figure 7-11. The curve is R1 at the bottom and from left to right R1 & R1' at the top. Note that R1' is read R1-prime.

Start the next ridge line by moving two longitudinal segments from the original starting point at the bottom. When the second one is done, move over two more segments and repeat. Since the s-curves are sketched by hand, they are not going to be identical. That is okay and actually desirable because it will be less monotonous than a uniform and precise one. In fact, to add a little uniqueness, vary where the branches occur. Label these last two sets of curves in an analogous manner to the first set using R2 and R3 and R2' and R3'.

At this point, it is worth trying to get a mental picture of how the ridge lines will be formed. In order to form a ridge line there needs to be a valley line on both sides. A cut is made on both sides of a ridge line down to the adjacent valley line. This leaves the ridge high and gives the desired effect. So now, the valley lines need to be drawn. Start by making tick marks half way between the longitudinal lines at the top and at the bottom. These marks will help establish where the valley lines go. At the top, draw radial lines to each one of these tick marks.

To establish the first valley line start at the point where R1 and R1' branch. Sketch an s-curve from this point to the tick mark halfway between R1 and R1'. This line is labeled VR1 and is shown in red in figure 7-12. Use a different color for the valley lines to minimize confusion when carving.

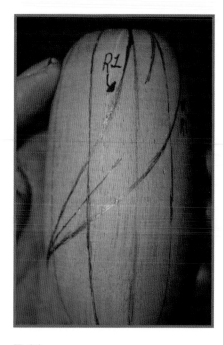

7-11 The branched curve is a ridge line and will remain high. Label the two branches R1 and R1' (read: R1-prime). This is the first of three-branched ridge lines.

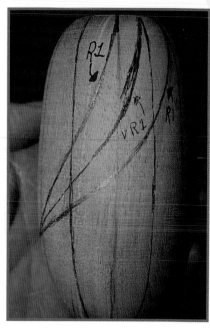

7-12 There is a valley line, labeled VR1 in red, between the two branches of the ridge line. This valley line starts at the branch point and terminates at the top half way between the two ridge lines.

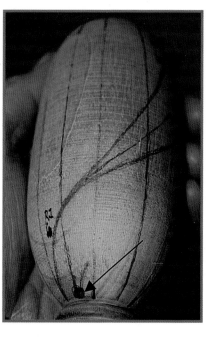

7-13 Begin a valley line at the point indicated. The valley line will be an s-curve that parallels the ridge line.

7-14 The valley line labeled V1 goes all the way to the top.

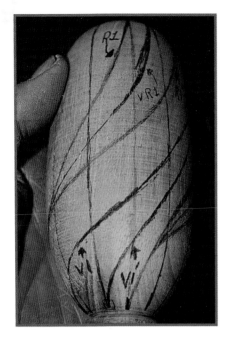

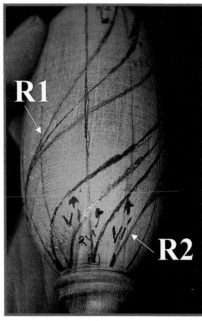

7-15 Note where the valley line V1′ starts relative to V1. Note also how it converges toward V1. It will intersect V1 before reaching the top of the blank.

7-16 Draw a ridge line from the point halfway between V1 and V1′ at the bottom to the intersection of V1 and V1′. Label this ridge line RV1.

7-17 Use a v-tool to cut the length of the valley lines. This shows early progress.

7-18 Iteratively deepen the valley and relieve each side back to the adjacent ridge line. Do this in several passes. Intermediate progress is shown here.

The next steps will establish two valley lines between two adjacent branched ridge lines. Hold the blank so the top points away and R1 is visible and on the left. Start at the bottom to the right of R1 halfway between R1 and the longitudinal line immediately to the right. Figure 7-13 shows the orientation and the starting point marked in red. Sketch an s-curve from this point to the point at the top that is half way between R1′ and the longitudinal line immediately to its right. Label this line V1. Use the same drawing techniques as described earlier. Figure 7-14 shows this valley line V1. Now draw the second valley line. Start at the bottom to the left of R2 halfway between R2 and the longitudinal line immediately to its left. Sketch an s-curve from this point to the same termination at the top as V1. Intersect V1 somewhere before the top of the blank. Label this valley line V1′. Figure 7-15 shows V1′ drawn in red and labeled. Draw similar branched valley lines between the other two ridge line pairs. Vary the distance from the top where the two lines intersect.

Finally, draw a ridge line between the branches of the branched valley lines. This ridge-line will start at the bottom on the longitudinal line just to the right of one of the ridge lines. It will terminate at the branch point of the branched valley line. This line is labeled RV1 and is shown in figure 7-16. Note that this ridge line stops short of the top of the blank and its length depends upon the branch point in the branched valley line.

At this point, there are three branched ridge lines with a valley line between its branches. In addition, there are three branched valley lines with a ridge line between its branches. The branched ridge lines, and branched valley lines, alternate around the perimeter of the blank. For the layout to be complete and consistent there must be a valley line between two adjacent ridge-lines and a ridge line between any two adjacent valley lines. The layout is now complete and consistent.

The easiest way to visualize how the flame is carved is as a series of v-cuts along the valley curves with beveled sides up to the adjacent ridge lines. As a valley line flows into a ridge line the depth of the valley will decrease to zero as it meets the ridge line. Conversely, the height of a ridge will fall as it flows into a valley. Keep this in mind as the carving proceeds and it will make the flame more understandable as the ridges and valleys unfold.

Start on one of the valley lines between the two branches of a branched ridge line. Begin by running a v-tool the entire length of the valley line. Figure 7-17 shows the idea. Bevel into the valley from both sides. Deepen the valley and repeat until the bevel widens out to the ridge lines. Note that the valley line is deepest at the top and rises to the surface of the blank as it flows into the ridge line near the base of the flame. To form the bevels, use as flat a chisel as possible, with a straight one being preferable. This may not be workable all the time so use a

7-19 Further progress on opening the valley.

7-20 One of the valleys is now complete. Note that the each valley wall begins at the adjacent ridge line.

7-21 Now move to a branched valley line. The technique is the same as before with the complication that two valleys converge with a ridge between the two valleys. Note how the ridge fades into the valley.

7-22 Note how the ridge is developing between the two valleys. This ridge is the bottom portion of the one in figure 7-21.

#2 or a #3 if needed. Figure 7-18 shows early progress on deepening the valley and forming the beveled sides. Figure 7-19 shows intermediate progress and figure 7-20 shows completed valley.

Move to an adjacent valley line, which will be one of the branched ones. Repeat the previous steps to deepen the valley and bevel the sides up to the ridge lines. Note in this case, there are the two valley branches so work both of them down together. Note also that the ridge line between the valley branches will be at the blank's surface at the base and that the ridge will continually drop in height as it flows into the valley as it nears the top. Figures 7-21 through 7-25 show intermediate phases in the process.

At this point one-third of the flame is carved. Move to the next valley in turn and repeat the process. Figure 7-26 shows all three segments complete. Although neither necessary nor critical, note that the smaller intermediate ridge wedges terminate closer to the top as the flame is rotated clockwise. This is something that can be changed by altering where the corresponding valley branches intersect.

The carving will look better if the ridge and valley lines are crisp, uniform, continuous and smooth. Also, the ridge lines that flow into a valley should do so smoothly. Be mindful of these while carving to minimize cleanup afterward. If a ridge line does not flow smoothly into a valley, cut the pointed end of the ridge to flow into the valley and

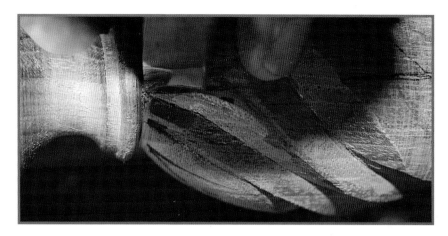

7-23 The ridge is starting to emerge. Use a skew chisel to get in the tight spaces near the base.

7-24 One of the branched valley lines is complete. This is a view of the base.

7-25 Another view of the same area. Note how the lines formed by the surfaces intersecting compare to the lines drawn on the blank in the beginning.

7-26 All of the valleys and ridges have been established. All that remains are some accent lines on each of the surfaces.

7-27 Draw 3 or 4 lines on each surface parallel to the edge of that surface. Use your finger as a guide to follow the edge.

blend the newly beveled surfaces into the existing ones.

The last step to this flame is to add some detail lines with a veiner. These accent lines are on every face of every lobe and run parallel to the outer edge in all cases. Use your finger as a guide to sketch the lines on the various surfaces of the flame. There will be three or four lines on each surface depending on the width. Figure 7-27 shows the technique and the lines drawn on

the carved surfaces. Use a #11, 2mm gouge, and carve the lines. Begin on the outside and work inwards. To deepen the cuts, without widening them, follow-up with a #11, 1mm gouge. A deeper cut will generate a darker shadow. Figure 7-28 shows some of the detail lines complete. Carve the remainder and the flame is done.

7-28 A few of the carved accent lines. Complete the remaining ones and the flame is done.

Chapter 8
Newport Flame Finial

This chapter will describe how to carve a flame finial that was used to adorn large case pieces that were made in Newport, Rhode Island during the last quarter of the 18th century. Stylistically this flame is characterized by a symmetric spiral pattern that sits on top of a leaf covered urn. The image below shows three of these flames installed on a desk and a bookcase.

Often times a flame finial is comprised of two turned and carved elements. The flame is one turning and the urn another. These are then fitted together with a circular mortise and tenon joint. Figure 8-1 shows the turning profiles and how the parts fit together. Start by

turning two blocks of wood to the specifications shown in figure 8-1.

It makes no difference whether the flame is carved first or second. I will start with the flame. Some layout and understanding is needed before carving begins. First, divide the

height of the flame blank into four equal parts by drawing three latitudinal lines equally spaced. These can be drawn while the blank is still on the lathe, or by hand afterwards. Next draw four longitudinal lines equal distances apart. These don't have to be perfect so sighting them

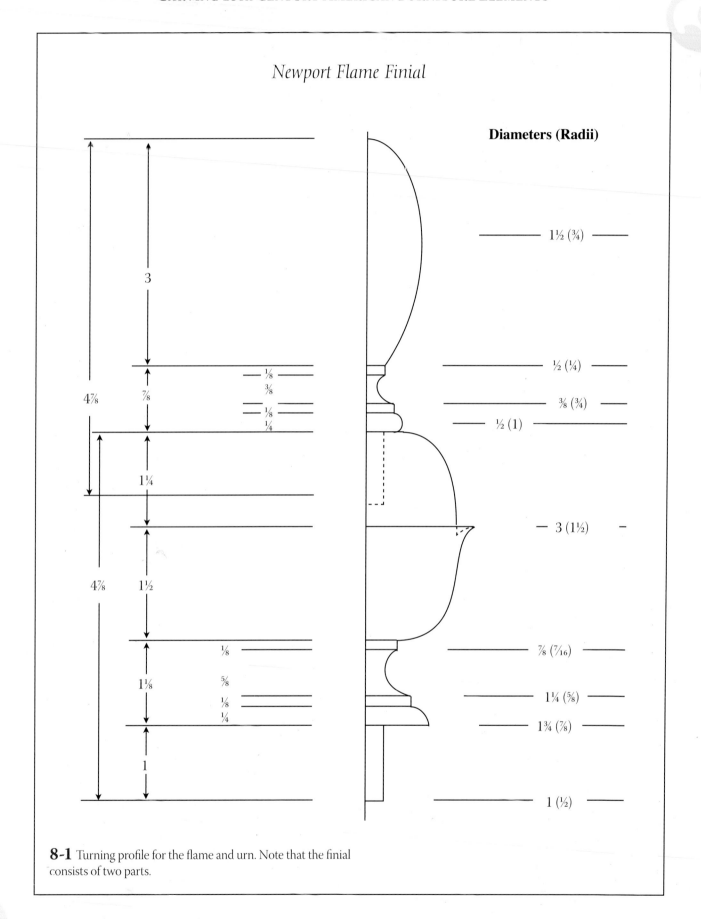

Newport Flame Finial

Diameters (Radii)

3

4⅞

7⅞

⅛
3⅜
⅛
¼

1¼

4⅞

1½

⅛

1⅛

⅝

⅛
¼

1

1½ (¾)

½ (¼)

⅜ (¾)

½ (1)

3 (1½)

⅞ (⁷⁄₁₆)

1¼ (⅝)

1¾ (⅞)

1 (½)

8-1 Turning profile for the flame and urn. Note that the finial consists of two parts.

8-2 Hold the blank as shown because it is easier to sight a straight line from the top to the bottom.

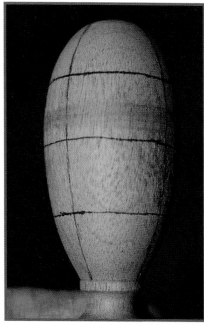

8-3 The lines of latitude and longitude divide the blank into four segments top to bottom and side to side to side.

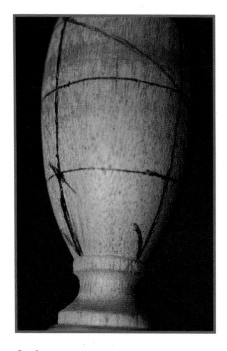

8-4 Draw a spiral from the bottom to the top beginning and ending on the same line of longitude while making one revolution. Pass through the intersection points as shown to generate the spiral line.

8-5 All four spiral lines are complete.

by eye is sufficient. One technique that might be helpful in drawing the line straight is to sight down the length of the flame blank instead of at ninety degrees to it. Figure 8-2 shows the technique. Figure 8-3 shows the longitudinal and latitudinal lines.

Next, sketch a spiral curve that will start at the base on a line of longitude and terminate at the top on the same line of longitude after making one revolution around the blank. As the spiral moves up and around the blank, it passes through the intersection point of the next line of latitude and line of longitude until it reaches the top. Figure 8-4 shows the start of one of the spiral curves. Draw three more spiral lines parallel to the first, beginning at the other three base longitudinal lines. Figure 8-5 shows all four spirals. The spiral lines just drawn will remain high and become ridge lines while the material between consecutive ones will be removed.

Secure the flame blank in a clamp and use a #9, 13mm gouge, to carve a trough down the center between two adjacent spiral lines as far as possible without turning the blank. I support the base of the flame with a block that has a ½-inch hole drilled in it. This gives more bearing surface on the clamp face, and the flame base, as well as extending the length in the clamp. Figure 8-6 shows the clamping mechanism and the first cut. Make another pass, or two, moving closer to the spiral lines. The ridge lines can become fragile as the scoop cuts get closer, especially when the ridge is running across

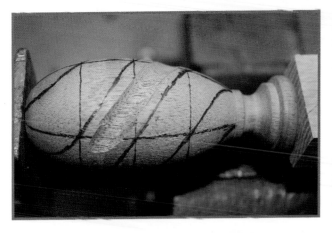

8-6 Use a scrap block with a ½-inch hole drilled in it to give a better clamping surface for the flame blank. Start to carve between adjacent spirals with a #9, 13mm gouge.

8-7 The spiral lines will be ridge lines. Use a #49 rasp to uniformly widen the trough between adjacent spirals. It is easier to get a blended surface with a rasp than the carving tool.

8-8 More progress in removing material between two spiral lines. Note how the trough tapers at the top of the blank.

8-9 Further blend and smooth the troughs with some sandpaper backed by a rubber, round, sanding block. Using your finger to support the sandpaper works just as well.

the grain. To minimize the chance of breakage along a ridge line, use a rasp and file to feather the surface into the ridge. It is even possible to break the ridge by running the file into it so start the file cut close to the ridge line and run it into the trough. Figure 8-7 shows this technique. It will take several passes to cleanly define the ridge. Figure 8-8 shows a completed section. The goal is to form crisp and clean spiral ridges connected with smooth and uniform troughs. Turn the flame and complete the shaping using

the same techniques. Clean up the surfaces with some sandpaper around a circular sanding block as shown in figure 8-9. Figure 8-10 shows all spirals complete and figure 8-11 shows the view from the top.

The urn is next. This particular urn has twenty leaf petals around its perimeter at the base. Divide the circumference around the top leaf section into twenty equal parts. Take a narrow piece of paper and wrap it around the perimeter at the top of the leaf section. Mark the

circumference on the paper. Remove the paper and divide this distance into twenty parts. If it doesn't divide evenly, by eye distribute the remaining distance over a couple of petals. Wrap the paper around the urn again and transfer the division marks onto the urn. Figure 8-12 shows this technique and result. Sketch in a straight line down the side of the urn to its base.

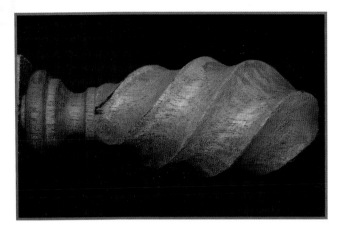

8-10 The full height of the completed flame.

8-11 A view from the top.

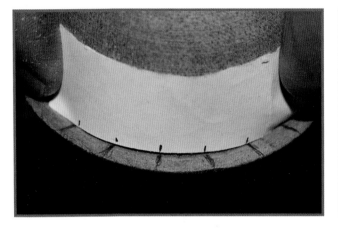

8-12 Divide the perimeter distance into twenty parts. If the perimeter does not divide evenly into twenty segments do one of two things. Either distribute the leftover distance among a few of the neighboring petals. The eye will not pick up slight differences in width. Or, leave the remaining section blank. This was routinely done in the 18th century.

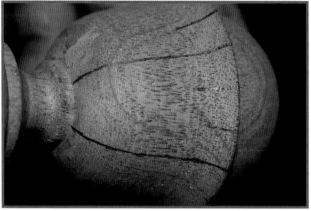

8-13 Sight the extension of the marks made in the previous step to the bottom of the urn. Draw the lines as shown. To help with uniform spacing draw two lines three divisions apart as shown. Then, by eye, divide the bottom section into three parts and draw the intermediate lines.

Move three marks to one side and draw another line down the side of the urn. Draw the line by sighting down the urn from top to bottom. Figure 8-13 shows the first two lines. Now sight and draw two additional lines corresponding to the marks at the top in between these first two. The eye should easily be able to split the distance at the urn base into thirds. Repeat this process until all the lines are drawn around the urn. These lines will be the petal separators. Finally, with your finger as a guide, draw a horizontal line around the outside of the urn as shown in figure 8-20. This line is approximately ⅛ of an inch down from the top and it will be the bottom of the "V" cuts that will separate the tips of the petals.

The layout is now complete. The carving strategy will be to first separate adjacent leaves and then detail each leaf. Begin to separate two adjacent leaves by making a "V" cut along one of the longitudinal lines down to the horizontal one. Figure 8-15 shows a couple of these cuts along with the technique. Do not make the entire "V" cut in one pass. Make several light passes and tap gently with a mallet. Because the wood in this area has been undercut, it is quite fragile and very susceptible to breakage. A heavy hit with the mallet even with a light cut could still cause a break.

After a sufficient number of the "V" cuts have been made, separate the remaining length with a small v-tool or a #11, 0.5mm gouge. Because this carving is especially repetitive, there

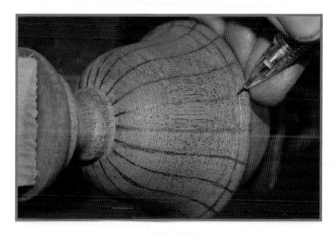

8-14 Draw a line around the perimeter approximately ⅛ of an inch down as shown. This line will be the depth of the "V" cuts that separate the tips of the petals.

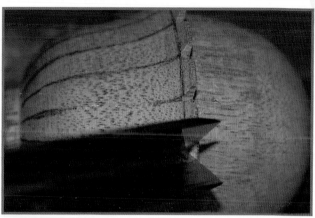

8-15 Begin to separate the petals using a v-tool. Make several shallow cuts and tap lightly with a mallet. The wood is quite weak on the edge and susceptible to breakage.

8-16 Use the v-tool to separate the leaves down the face of the urn.

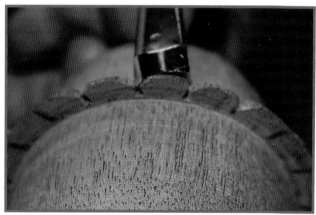

8-17 Round the petal tips with a #7, 10mm gouge.

is some flexibility in the order of operations. That is, all of the petal tip separating cuts could be made before moving to the next stage or one entire leaf could be worked on to completion. For this discussion I will work a few to completion and leave it to the reader to repeat the process for the remainder of the urn. Figure 8-16 shows a couple of these cuts completed and the technique used. Next, round the tips of each petal with a #7, 10mm gouge. Round from the base of a "V" cut to the center of a petal on each side. Figure 8-17 shows the technique and figure 8-18 shows the results. Again, to

avoid breakage, it is better to take a few light cuts than one large one.

The petals are now separated and the tips rounded. Now each petal will be detailed by scooping out the center from top to bottom. Use the largest #9 gouge that will fit. In this case, it was a 13mm. Scoop out the center and leave a uniform perimeter around the edge. Figure 8-19 shows the technique and a partially completed petal. As the petal narrows toward the bottom, the cut will become shallower and only a small portion of the cutting edge will be used. The goal is to get a uniform

perimeter around the edge of the petal which means that the scooped portion will be wider at the top and it will taper as it flows to the bottom of the urn. The more uniform and smooth these two items are determines the success of the carving.

Finally, clean up the edges of each petal with a riffler file. A riffler file is a small file typically with a bent end and shaped to some profile. They usually come in a set of 8 or more with a variety of profiles. These are very useful for cleanup work on a variety of carvings. For this operation, I like one that is curved

8-18 A few of the petals are rounded.

8-19 Detail each petal by scooping out the center with a #9, 13mm gouge. Strive for a narrow, uniform perimeter around each petal.

8-20 Use a riffler with a "V" profile to clean up the separation lines and blend them into the rounded tips.

and comes to a "V" at the bottom. Figure 8-20 shows the tool and the technique. To finish the urn carving repeat the process on the remaining petals. Figure 8-21 shows what the urn and flame will look like when completed and finished.

8-21 A completed flame and urn.

Chapter 9
Convex Newport Shell

The blockfront furniture that was built by the Townsends and Goddards in Newport, Rhode Island in the last quarter of the 18th century is some of the most admired and iconic designs yet created. The unique shell motifs that are extremely well integrated into those designs are a significant reason for their continued popularity. There are two versions of the Newport shell. One is concave and is always carved from the solid into a drawer front, desk slant front or a door. The other is convex and is most often applied. Typically, the shells are used in groups of three, with a central concave one flanked by two convex ones. Figures 9-1 and 9-1A show two typical applications. This chapter will describe how to carve the convex version and the next will concentrate on the concave one.

9-1 The convex shell presented in this chapter is sized to be one of those applied to the top drawer of this kneehole bureau. Note how the convex shell tops off, and terminates, the vertical blocking on each side.

The convex shell was designed to top off a blocked, raised panel. In some cases, a portion of the blocked element is integral with the shell and in others the shell is slightly under-cut at the bottom and fits over the contoured top of the blocked panel. This chapter will describe how to layout and carve a shell with a portion of the panel connected. The size of this shell is what would be found on a blockfront, kneehole bureau such as the one in figure 9-1.

Start with a 1-inch thick blank 9 inches (w) x 5¼ inches (h) as specified in figure 9-2. Use a compass to draw the circular arcs centered at the point labeled "X" as shown in figure 9-3. The two arcs shown in figure 9-3 are the outer most and the inner most ones from figure 9-2. Then, use a square to draw

9-1A Typical shell applications.

the vertical lines as shown. With the point of a compass, match the center point from figure 9-2 to the center point in figure 9-3. Use carbon paper to transfer the bottom curves and central medallion. Note the faint tick marks around the perimeter of the medallion. These are the ends of the lobe separation lines. They will be needed later to draw these lines after some sculpting has been done. Now turn the blank upside down and draw the shell perimeter as shown in figure 9-4. This will be used as a guide later.

Next, use a bandsaw to cut the blank as shown it figure 9-5. Set a marking gauge to ⅝ of an inch and scribe a line measured from the back as shown in figure 9-6. The bottom portion of the blank has rounded edges as shown in figure 9-2. Make a template of this corner and transfer the shape to the bottom of the blank as shown in figure 9-7. The results are shown in figure 9-8. Note that the top is up and the bottom is down.

The next step is to remove the material above the line in figure 9-8 underneath the bottom curve as viewed from the top. Begin by setting in along the bottom curve on the top surface as shown in figure 9-9. Figure 9-10 shows early progress and figure 9-11 shows the operation complete. Note that the edges still need to be rounded. Figure 9-12 shows the layout for the edges. Set in around the curved line, round the edge with a flat chisel and cleanup with a file. Figure 9-13 shows this result. Make sure the rounded surface is square to the bottom edge. Figure

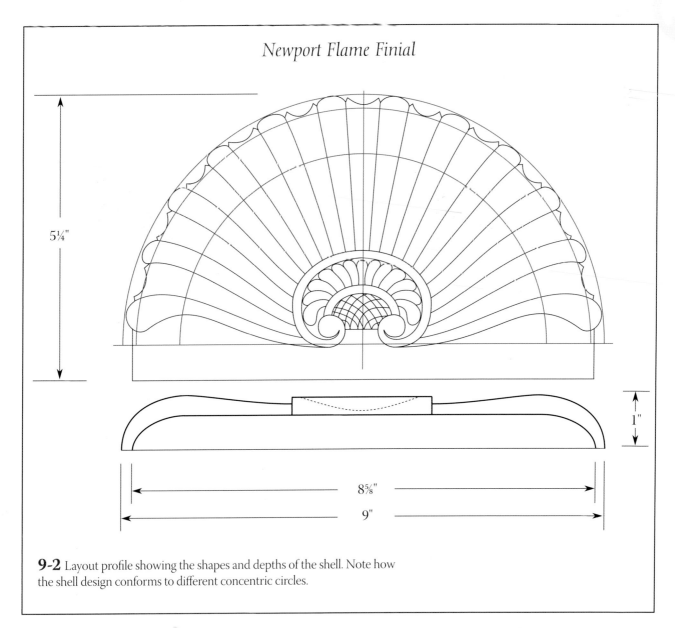

Newport Flame Finial

5¼"

1"

8⅝"

9"

9-2 Layout profile showing the shapes and depths of the shell. Note how the shell design conforms to different concentric circles.

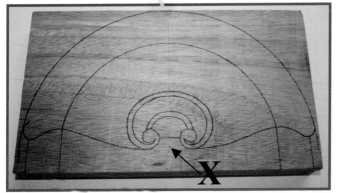

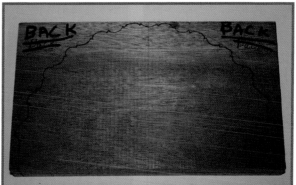

9-3 Use a compass, with the center as marked, to draw the circles shown. Then match up the centers of the drawing in figure 9-2 with the center on the blank and draw the bottom curve as well as the central medallion. Use carbon paper for the transfer. Finally, use a square to place the vertical lines as shown.

9-4 Use a compass and the same relative center as on the front to draw the outside circle. The inner one is not needed on the back. Use carbon paper and transfer the outside profile of the shell. This will be used as a guide for carving.

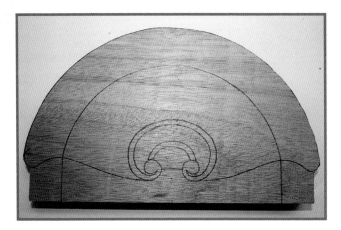

9-5 Cut out the outer profile using a bandsaw.

9-6 Use a marking gauge set to ⅝ of an inch and scribe a line on the bottom edge using the back as the reference surface.

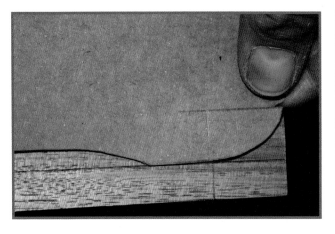

9-7 On the bottom edge, trace the rounded edge profile. Make a template for this shape based on the information in figure 9-2.

9-8 The blank as viewed from the bottom edge. The material on top will be removed so the bottom will be a rounded edge rectangle.

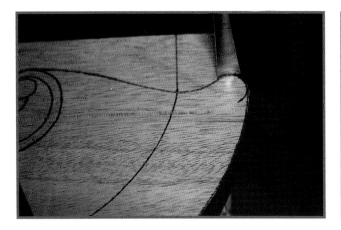

9-9 Begin to set in along the curve at the bottom on the front face. Do not undercut this edge. Ideally, the cut would be 90°, but err on the side of having the base flair out as opposed to an undercut.

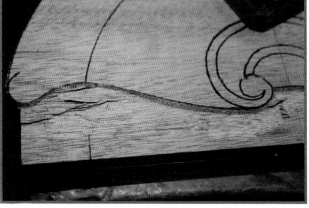

9-10 More progress on removing the wood below the curve down to the bottom.

9-11 The operation is complete and the shell is now "raised" above the background.

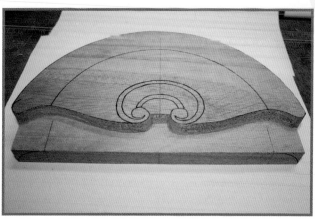

9-12 Next, remove the rounded corners. Use a flat chisel, rasp and file for this. Note that the rounded edge will blend into the flat area at the vertical line.

9-13 Most of the corner is rounded.

9-14 Check that the surface of the rounded area is square to the bottom edge. If it is not, remove material until it is. Note that more material near the base of the curve needs to be removed.

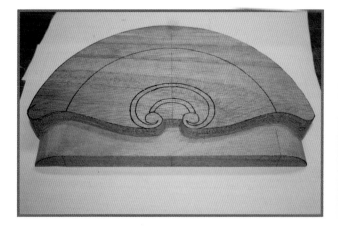

9-15 Both edges are rounded. Next, sculpt the shell to the proper shape.

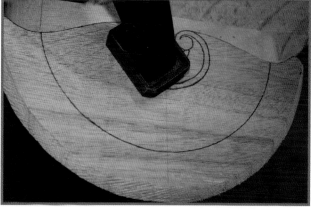

9-16 First, round over the outer circular perimeter from the inner circle down to the back face of the blank. Use a #49 rasp for this. This picture shows early progress in rounding the perimeter.

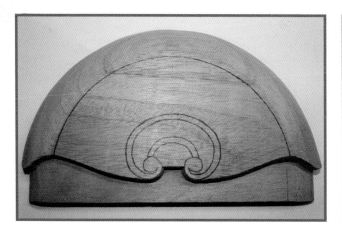

9-17 The edge is sufficiently rounded. Note that the inner circle remains high.

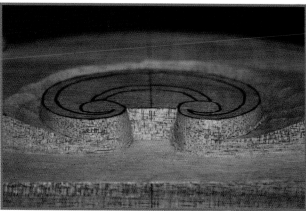

9-18 Set in around the central medallion and remove the wood behind the cut. Use a #5, 12mm gouge, for the removal operation and use the appropriate 2's, 3's and 5's for the set in.

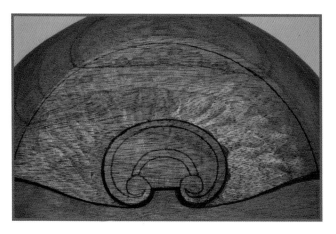

9-19 Blend the background into the high spot at the inner circular arc. Use #3 and #2 gouges for this operation.

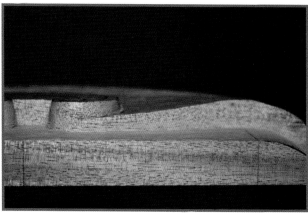

9-20 This is the view from the bottom. Notice the smooth and uniform surface that flows up from the medallion, over the top and down to the back.

9-14 shows the edge is not square. Remove material near the base of the curve to bring the rounded edge into square. Figure 9-15 shows both edges rounded.

Now round over the top circular portion from the inner circle down to the back surface at the perimeter. The idea here is to round over the edge similar to the base portion just completed, only along the circular perimeter. Use a #49 rasp for this operation. Figure 9-16 shows early progress. Figure 9-17 shows the rounding complete.

Next, raise the central medallion by lowering the background around it to approximately ¼ of an inch. Begin by setting in around the perimeter as shown in figure 9-18. The gouges that match the curvature will be #5's, #3's and #2's. Blend the background surface from the inner arc into the medallion keeping the arc high. Use larger #5's and #3's and strive for a smoothly flowing surface. Figure 9-19 shows the operation complete. Figure 9-20 shows the profile of the surface and figure 9-21 shows another view of the sculpted surface. The goal is to get a smooth, blended

surface that is low near the medallion, rises up to a high point at the inner circle and then falls off down to the bottom.

The overall shape of the shell is now complete. What remains is to add the details. The first detail to add will be the lobes that make up the majority of the shell. In an earlier step, the jagged perimeter was drawn on the back. Sketch marks on the circular edge at the points illustrated in figure 9-22. The marks will be one end of the separation lines between the convex and concave lobes. Connect

81

9-21 This is the view from the top. Notice that the inner circular arc is the high spot of the surface.

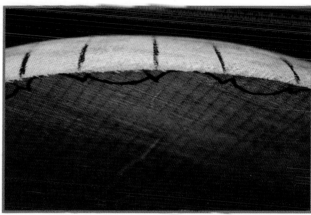

9-22 Use the shell outline on the back to position the lobe separation lines on the perimeter. Align them with the extension of the bisector of the angle between the adjacent lobes.

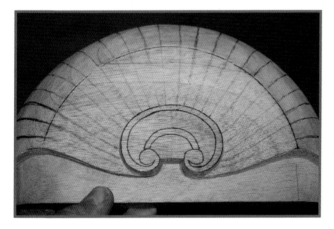

9-23 Sketch in the lobe separators by connecting the marks made at the perimeter with the marks on the central medallion. Recall that ends of the lobe separators were marked on the central medallion when it was transferred from the template. The lines are drawn freehand.

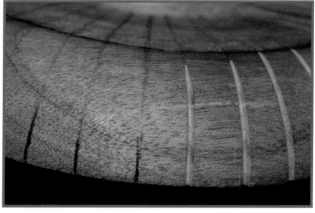

9-24 Begin separating the lobes by carving with a v-tool along the lines just drawn.

these ends with the corresponding marks that were drawn on the central medallion earlier. Figure 9-23 shows these lines drawn on the front of the blank. There should be twenty-two separation lines since there are twenty-three lobes on this shell. If this is not the case, work out what is wrong now or there will be no good way to correct this later.

Of the twenty-three lobes around the circular perimeter of this shell, twelve are convex and eleven concave. Starting at the bottom with a convex one and alternating with the concave ones the pattern concludes with a convex one on the bottom on the other side. There are only two unique elements to be carved. Start by cutting with a small v-tool along the separation lines as shown in figure 9-24. Continue the "V" cut following the line all the way to the medallion. Round over the edge on the convex side and leave the wall alone on the concave side. Figure 9-25 shows intermediate progress shaping a couple of the convex lobes. Make sure that the wall on the concave side is about 90° to the base of the convex one. Figure 9-26 shows the angle. It will take a few iterations with the v-tool and rounding to get to the desired depth. Use the profile on the back as a guide for the depth of the "V" cuts. Figure 9-27 shows a couple of the convex lobes complete with the intermediate concave ones ready to be carved.

Now work on one of the concave lobes. Scooping out the center with a series of #9 gouges shapes the

9-25 Deepen the v-cut and round over the edge on the convex lobe side. This shows intermediate progress shaping a couple of the convex lobes.

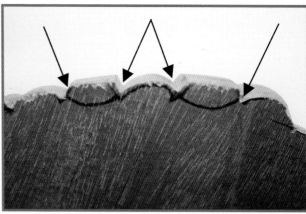

9-26 Use the shell outline on the back as a guide for the depth of the v-cuts. Also, note the angle the concave lobe makes with the adjacent convex one. The angle is approximately 90°.

9-27 A couple of convex lobes are now complete. Use files, scrapers and sandpaper as needed to get a smooth and uniform surface.

9-28 Use the outline on the back as a guide to shaping the concave lobes. In this case, do not be a slave to the outline. If the lobe looks good and doesn't match the guide go with what looks good.

concave lobes. Use wider chisels such as a 13mm or a 10mm one for the wider areas and a 5 or 7mm one for the narrower areas. In the narrow portions take very light cuts because there is not a lot of material to remove. A definite yet shallow contour is desired. As shown in figure 9-28, use the drawing on the back as a guide. In the case of these concave shapes let the tool define the curvature and don't be a slave to the guide lines. They are just guides so use them as such. If the curve looks good, don't worry that

it doesn't match the guide exactly. Figure 9-29 shows a completed concave lobe.

Here are a couple of things to keep in mind as the lobes are being shaped. First, the ends of all of the lobes are fragile on the perimeter at the bottom. Thus, they are very susceptible to chip out. One way to avoid this is not to cut straight down at the bottom. Use a file to shape the ends as shown in figure 9-30. Second, because there will be significant grain change in some of

the lobes, a file can also be used to help uniformly and safely shape the separating "V" grooves between two adjacent lobes. A file that works well is a "V" shaped riffler or a similarly shaped detail as the one shown in figure 9-31. Use a v-tool to make the initial cut to define a channel. Finish with the shaped file if needed. Complete the remainder of the lobes using the same techniques. This will take some time because there are so many of them, but there is nothing new about them.

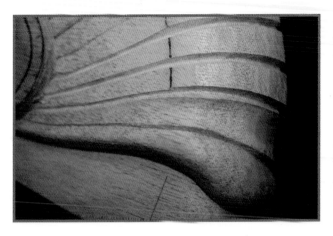

9-29 A convex and a concave lobe are now complete. Shape the remaining lobes using the same techniques.

9-30 Because the wood at the base of the perimeter is fragile due to grain direction, it is best not to cut all the way through from the top. Use a half round file to shape the end of the concave lobes.

9-31 Use a v-profiled file to refine and deepen the separation grooves. This is a safe and effective method to fine-tune the angle of the concave lobe edge.

9-32 Begin to lower the area below the inner half-ring by setting in along the line as shown. Use a #3, 8mm gouge, for this operation.

9-33 Use a #7, 6mm gouge, around the buttons.

9-34 Remove material down approximately ³⁄₁₆ of an inch. Deepen the perimeter and carve down around the perimeter, leaving the center high.

9-35 The center is the high spot and the surface falls off in all directions.

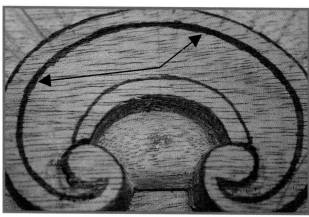

9-36 Widen the specified line toward the center as shown. Then gently set in on the outside of the line. There is to be v-cut along the entire length of the specified line.

9-37 Use the corner of a flat chisel to slice from the inside portion of the line into the base of the set in cut. This will form one leg of a "v".

9-38 One leg of the "v" is now complete.

The last item to be carved on this shell is the central medallion. There is a lot of detail in this small area so some of the carving will be in tight spaces, which is a complication, and most of the elements are small so the cuts need to be delicate and precise, which is another complication. This is not meant to be frightening, but just a reminder to be careful. Start by setting in along the lines as shown in figures 9-32 and 9-33. Use a #3, 8mm gouge, for the flatter curve and a #7, 6mm one for the tighter curves. Remove the material as shown in figure 9-34 down about

⁄₁₆ of an inch. Now set in a little deeper around the perimeter of this space. Leave the center high and carve down into the set in cuts on all sides. The goal is to have a rounded dome shape that is high in the center and falls off in all directions. Finally, smooth out any facets left by the carving tools. Figure 9-35 shows the final shape. This area is done for now, but detail lines will be added as the last step.

The next operation is one of the most delicate cuts of the entire medallion. The perimeter ring needs

to be separated from the interior with a small "V" groove. That is, a "V" groove needs to be made along the line shown in figure 9-36. I prefer not to use a v-tool for this operation because the grain changes dramatically around the perimeter and I want to avoid tear out as much as possible. To that end, first thicken the perimeter line by using a fatter pencil or sketching near it. Widen the line towards the center because there is more material on that side. Figure 9-36 also shows this line widened by a sufficient amount. Now delicately set in at 90° along the

85

9-39 Set in around the outer edge of the inner half-ring and remove the material behind it as shown.

9-40 Form a smooth surface as shown. Take the depth to approximately ⅛ of an inch. Use a #5, 12mm gouge, for most of the shaping. A small #7 will probably be needed around the buttons. The surface is now complete.

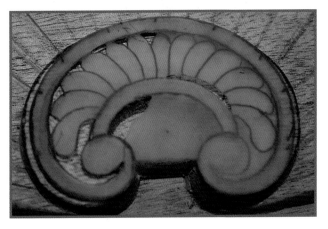

9-41 Make a separate template of the central medallion as shown. Note that the tops of the petals are cut out on half and the bottoms are on the other. This allows the template to remain intact while still being able to transfer the needed information. Trace through the openings available. Make tick marks at the petal dividing lines at the bottom on the right.

9-42 Flip the template side to side and repeat.

outside of the line using a #3 or a #5 gouge. Bevel from the inside of the line into the base of the set in cut as shown in figure 9-37. A technique that works well in delicate areas is to use the corner of a flat, or relatively flat, chisel and move the tool in a slicing motion. This requires little pressure so the chance of breakage is minimized. The goal is to have an angled ramp around the perimeter. This is needed to support the central section because it is going to be

carved further and without the support, the edges would be fragile and likely to break. Figure 9-38 shows the perimeter carved with an angled side on the interior portion.

Now this central portion is going to be contoured by leaving the perimeter high and falling off as it flows towards its center. The area around the button ends requires delicate treatment. Set in along the lines as shown in figure 9-39 and remove the

background behind these cuts. Be careful near the points indicated in figure 9-39. This is the most delicate area because the surfaces come to a point in a small and tight location. Once this area is carved the remaining items are comparatively easy. The height of the inner half-ring should be about ⅛ of an inch. Leaving the outer perimeter high, blend the surface into the depth established at the inner half-ring. Figure 9-40 shows the operation complete.

9-43 The left-hand side shows what is left after tracing the template. The right hand side shows how to connect the lines to form the petals.

9-44 All of the petals are drawn. These are done freehand.

9-45 Widen the outline of each petal towards the center. The petals are to rest on top of the underlying surface. Thus, the tops cannot consume the entire background.

9-46 Gently set in around the petal tops as shown and then remove wood behind them back to the perimeter line. This is where the v-cut made earlier is important. The angled drop off provides good support for the high ridge. If the drop off were vertical, or undercut, the ridge would have little or no support and would be much more vulnerable to breakage.

Next, a series of petals will be carved on top of the surface just established. Make a separate template of the medallion as shown in figure 9-41. Trace around the cut out areas. On the right, just above the inner half-ring make little tick marks that place the ends of the various petals. Then flip the template side to side as shown in figure 9-42 and trace the same cut out areas. Note that this time the open areas are opposite of what they were previously. The left

side of figure 9-43 shows what the results of the tracings are and the right side shows how these are connected to form the petals. These petals are best sketched freehand. Figure 9-44 shows the petals drawn. It is now time to separate the individual petals and then finally to detail each one of them.

Begin to separate the petals by first thickening the outlines as shown in figure 9-45. Thicken them towards

the center. The reason for this is that there needs to be a little margin around the top of each petal. If the edge went right to the end of the underlying surface, that surface would be completely removed. The goal is to have the petals appear to rest on top of the cupped inner surface. Thus, there needs to be some margin around the tips of the petals. Carefully set in along the inside edge of the thickened line around the petal perimeters and remove

87

9-47 More progress outlining the tops of the petals. Be careful and use small tools to remove the material behind the petals. It is important to keep the ridge line a nice gentle curve or it will not look good.

9-48 Separate the petals with a small v-tool.

9-49 Detail each petal by scooping the center with a #9, 13mm gouge. Use the center of the tool and strive to get a gentle trough that goes from side to side. These troughs will not be deep.

9-50 Round the edges of the inner half-ring. Start by drawing a centerline.

material behind as shown in figures 9-46 and 9-47. A #8, 4mm gouge, will fit many of the petal tops. Use whatever small chisels will work. Remember to leave the outer edge of the underlying surface high. This will allow the petals to sit on top of that surface.

Next, separate each petal. Use a small v-tool to carve along the pencil lines previously drawn. Figure 9-48 shows some of the lines

and some of them carved. Finally, detail each petal by gently scooping the center with a #9 gouge. I used the center portion of a #9, 13mm gouge, but a 10mm one would work just as well. Figure 9-49 shows the detailed petals. Strive for a gentle curve from side to side the entire length of the petal. Don't get too deep, otherwise the edges of the petals will be fragile and likely to break.

The edges of the inner half-ring will now be rounded. Draw a centerline as shown in figure 9-50. Use a flat chisel as shown in figure 9-51 to knock off the edges. Scrape, file and sand to make the surface round and uniform so any cross-section is a semi-circle. Now, in a similar manner, round over the outer ring of the medallion. Start by drawing a centerline as shown in figure 9-52. First, use a flat chisel to knock off the corners on the outside edge.

9-51 Use a small flat chisel to slice off the edge. Use a file or scraper to clean up the facets left by the chisel.

9-52 Draw a centerline before rounding over the outer ring.

9-53 Round the outer ring of the medallion. Draw the centerline and then slice off the edge as before.

9-54 Smooth the facets as before. Use the flat chisel as a scraper to get into tight areas. The outer ring is now complete.

Continue the rounding into and around the terminating button. Take shallower cuts on the button because the edges are less high. Figure 9-53 shows progress with the outer edge. Successively remove the edges formed by the previous operation until the outer surface is facet free. Use a small file to do the intermediate and final blending. Using similar techniques round over the inner edge. This operation is more delicate than the work on the outside edges

because the depth is much less. Use a flat chisel to take off the corner and then use it as a scraper to blend the edges. Figure 9-54 shows the outer ring complete.

Finally, a few detail lines will be carved into the lowered central dome. Draw hatch lines as shown in figure 9-55. Use a small v-tool to carve along the lines. Be careful of the grain and the feel of the chisel because it is easy to break off a piece.

If the chisel offers too much resistance come from the other direction rather than just pushing harder. Figure 9-56 shows the hatch lines complete.

That completes the unique items on this shell. Complete the concave and convex lobes and the shell is ready to attach to a drawer front. Figure 9-57 shows a completed and finished convex shell.

9-55 Draw hatch marks as shown. Use a small v-tool and carve along the hatch lines. Be careful of the grain because the wood can be fragile here. Do not force a cut. If there is too much resistance come from the other direction.

9-56 The hatch lines are completely carved.

9-57 Here is a completed and finished version of the convex shell. Note how the light forms a semi-circle as it reflects off the high spots. This is the desired effect.

Chapter 10
Concave Newport Shell

As mentioned in the previous chapter the concave shell was designed to compliment the convex one. In this context, the compliment of a raised block terminated by a convex shell is a sunken panel, or cut out, terminated by a concave shell. The size of the shell presented in this chapter is designed to fit the door in a blockfront kneehole bureau, such as my version in figure 10-1.

Figure 10-2 shows the pattern that will used in this chapter. Trace the front view of the pattern onto the blank of wood as shown in figure 10-3. In addition, use a compass to draw the circular arc inside the shell edge. This is also shown in figure 10-3. Next, draw the bottom view as shown in figure 10-4. The two patterns on the blank together are shown figure 10-5. Note that the blank that I am using for this discussion is shorter than it would be for a real project. All the concepts are the same with the exception that the scooped area below the shell would be taller. Start the carving with the bottom of the shell. Set in along the curved line at the bottom of the shell as shown in figure 10-6. Be careful not to affect the volute walls since they are quite thin and fragile. Theoretically the set in cut should go perpendicular to the surface however, it works a little better if the base of the cut is a bit wider.

10-1 The concave shell presented in this chapter is sized to fit the door of this kneehole bureau. The door is located in the center between the two banks of drawers.

It is important not to undercut the surface. Figure 10-7 shows intermediate progress and figure 10-8 shows the area near the volute.

Figure 10-9 shows the corner cleaned up and figure 10-10 shows the bottom region complete.

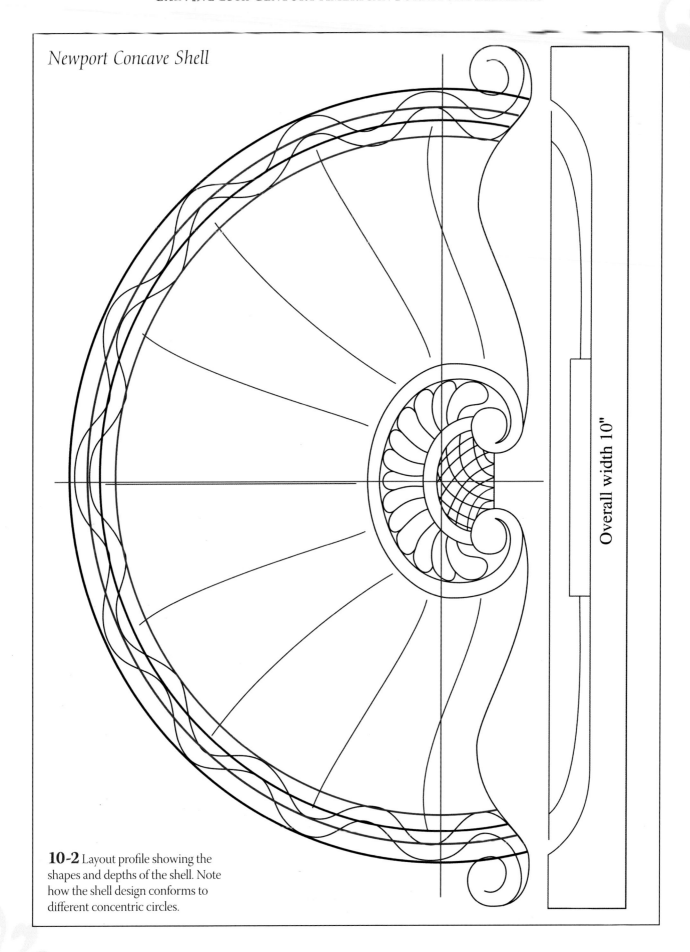

Newport Concave Shell

Overall width 10"

10-2 Layout profile showing the shapes and depths of the shell. Note how the shell design conforms to different concentric circles.

Now that the entire shell is separated from the background, it is time to sculpt the interior. The bottom view of figure 10-2 shows the cross sectional view of the shell as seen from the bottom. Note that the highest point of the central medallion is below the surface of the blank by ⅛ of an inch. With your finger as a guide, draw a line on the bottom vertical surface ⅛ of an inch from the top of the blank. Figure 10-11 shows this line. Feather down to this mark from the semi-circular arc that was drawn on the front of the blank. Figure 10-12 shows the circular arc along with the depth line. Start out using a large #5 or #7 then switch to a flatter gouge, such as a #3, 20-25mm and a #2, 20-25mm, as the depth is neared. Note that narrower gouges than these can be used so it is not necessary to buy bigger ones just for this operation. When the desired depth is reached smooth out the surface with a scraper and/or sandpaper. The surface does not have to be perfect, just smooth enough to be able to draw on it. Figures 10-13 through 10-16 show progressive stages and technique. Figures 10-17 and 10-18 show views of the completed operation.

Draw in the central medallion as shown in figure 10-19. Set in around the medallion and raise it up about ⅛ of an inch as shown in figure 10-20. Use the same tools and techniques as before. After the medallion has been raised, feather the background into the circular arc as before. Figure 10-21 shows the results of this operation. Sketch in centerlines for the concave lobes.

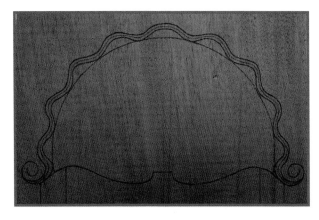

10-3 Use carbon paper to transfer the shell outline from figure 10-2 to the blank. Then use a compass to draw the interior circle. Finally, use a square to place the vertical lines as shown.

10-4 Draw the bottom profile on the blank as specified in figure 10-2. The depth of the sunken area is ½ of an inch.

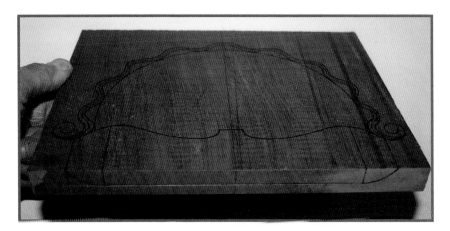

10-5 This shows how the front and bottom profiles interact.

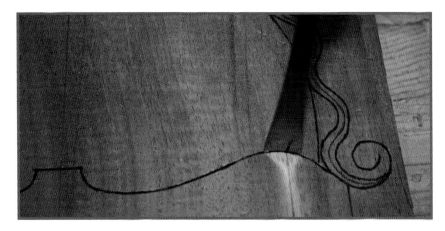

10-6 First, remove the material below the bottom curve. Begin this process by setting in along the curve as shown.

10-7 Early progress sculpting the sunken panel.

10-8 Note that the corner of the sunken area rises gradually to the top of the blank.

10-9 Use a #7 or #5 gouge to shape the corner.

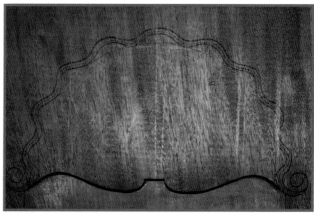

10-10 The bottom portion is complete.

10-11 Draw a line ⅛ of an inch below the top of the blank. The center of the shell will be sculpted to this line.

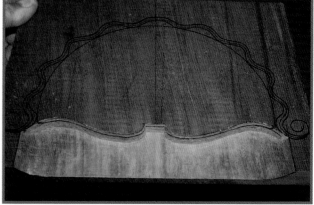

10-12 Remove the material bounded by the circular arc and the ⅛ inch line on the bottom edge.

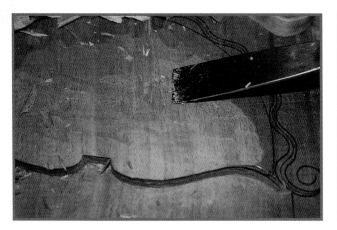

10-13 Intermediate progress sculpting the center.

10-14 Notice how the surface rises smoothly to the top of the blank inside the circular arc. Be mindful of the grain and reverse direction when needed.

10-15 Continued progress.

10-16 Use a #7, 16mm gouge to shape the circular perimeter.

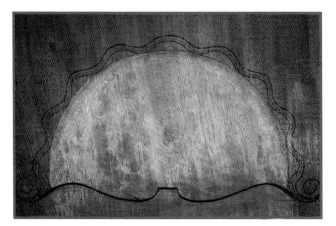

10-17 The center portion is now complete.

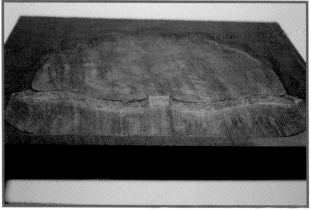

10-18 A view of the dished region from the bottom.

10-19 Use a separate template for the medallion to draw it in place. See the chapter on the convex shell for details on how to draw in the medallion details.

10-20 Set in around the medallion to a depth of ⅛ of an inch.

10-21 Blend the background uniformly to the circular arc.

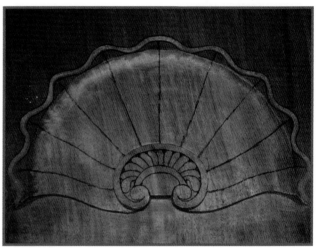

10-22 Sketch the centerlines of the concave lobes.

Use the tick marks around the outer perimeter of the central medallion as one end of these centerlines and the centers of lobes as shown in the figure 10-22 as the other. These will be used later after the perimeter is complete.

The next step is to carve the narrow outline around the perimeter. Note that the terminating volutes are even narrower than the rest of the perimeter outline. The majority of this outline detail is a "v-groove" that follows the profile of the shell. Keep this in mind as you carve. I do not use a v-tool to carve this groove. Rather I prefer to make a cut straight down the centerline and bevel into it from each side. I get a crisper line with this method than I would with a v-tool. In addition, it is easier to deal with changing grain direction.

Insert a centerline around the perimeter. This is best done by freehand. Blend this centerline into the terminating volute because it is easy to get confused here and make an errant cut. A missed cut in the delicate volute area poses a bigger problem than it might somewhere else because the cuts are close together so the space between them is small and fragile. Pay particular attention to how the centerline blends into the volute. Figure 10-23 shows an enlarged drawing of the terminating volute. Start carving

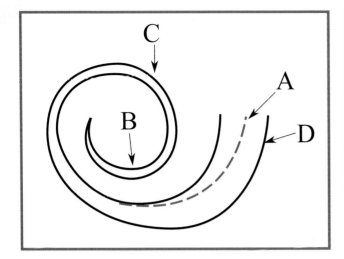

10-23 Enlarged view of the terminating scroll.

10-24 The perimeter is a v-groove that follows the undulating curve. Draw a centerline as shown in red. Set in along this line and bevel into it from each side.

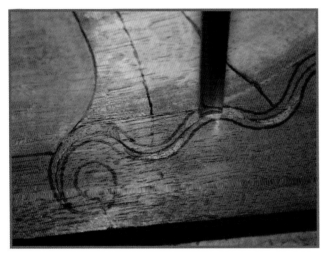

10-25 Use a gouge that is slightly tighter than the curve for a concave orientation.

10-26 Use a gouge that is slightly flatter than the curve for a convex orientation.

the perimeter away from the volutes and work into them later. With a #3, 8mm gouge, cut perpendicular to the wood along the centerline. Change to a #5, 8mm gouge, as the curvature of the line increases. Use a #2, 8mm gouge the line flattens out. There is no exact way to do this, just keep the goal in mind as you go. The curvature of the line will determine which gouge to use. Since this element is not very deep, hand pressure on the gouge is adequate

although a mallet would also work with light tapping. Figure 10-24 shows progress cutting along the centerline.

You could cut in the entire centerline and then bevel the sides, but I prefer to work on a smaller portion to completion, and then move to the next section. Because the centerline is an undulating curve with concave and convex curvature, the beveled sides falling into it will also alternate

between concave and convex. In fact, for any point along the length of the line, the curvature on one of the beveled sides will be concave and the side opposite at that point will be convex. When making a concave bevel use a slightly higher numbered gouge, that is a tighter radius, and when cutting a convex bevel use a lower numbered gouge, that is flatter radius. This will prevent the corners of the gouge from digging into the wall of the bevel. Figure

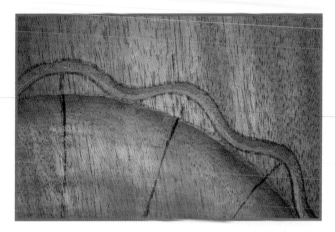

10-27 A section of the perimeter is complete. Note how both sides angle down into the centerline and how that centerline follows the undulating curve.

10-28 Note how the centerline flows into the thin terminating scroll.

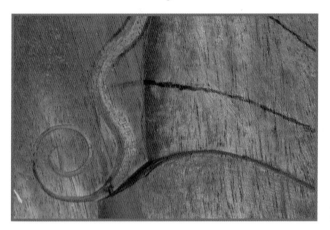

10-29 A completed scroll.

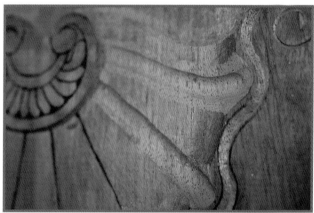

10-30 Use a #9, 10mm gouge, along the centerlines of the concave lobes.

10-31 Early progress on deepening the trough.

10-32 Round over the edges formed by the gouge cuts and blend the surfaces so they are smooth and continuous.

10-25 shows the concave technique and figure 10-26 shows the convex one. Figure 10-27 shows a section complete. Repeat this sequence along the remainder of the curve excluding the volute terminations.

Now concentrate on one of the terminating volutes. Refer again to figure 10-23, which is an enlarged drawing of one of the terminating volutes. Notice how the centerline A, blends into the inside line of the volute B, and the setback line C, blends into the inside line of the shell perimeter D. Carefully set in along line B and blend it into the centerline A. Bevel into this line from C and blend the surface into the inside wall. Finally feather the outside perimeter line E into B. Figure 10-28 shows intermediate progress and figure 10-29 shows the operation complete. The goal is to have crisp, smooth lines and uniform blended surfaces. Cleanup any facets with the flattest gouge that will work. For convex surfaces a flat chisel works well and a small #2 or #3 gouge is appropriate for concave ones. Repeat this process on the other side.

The next step is to separate and define the lobes. This will be a highly repetitive process of scooping a valley and rounding over the edges on each side and then repeating. Start with a #9, 10mm gouge and make an initial cut following the centerlines drawn earlier. Now follow-up with another pass to deepen the trough. Stay just shy of the perimeter at first and sneak up on it later. When the depth is such that the corners of the gouge are about to catch, round

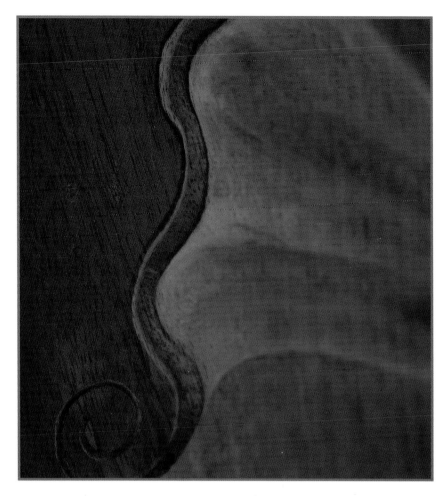

10-33 A couple of completed lobes. Note how the surface is smooth and continuous.

10-34 The completed central medallion. This medallion is identical to the one on the convex shell. See that chapter for details on how to carve it.

over the edges and then deepen and round some more. Figure 10-30 shows the initial cut and figure 10-31 shows early progress. Use a flat chisel to round over the edges. A backbent gouge can also be used for this, but it is not necessary. Grain direction will be a significant and constant issue during this whole process. When doing the scooping operation, one side of the tool will cut well and the other side will be more or less against the grain. Sometimes this will not be a huge problem and nothing special need be done. Other times this will be a big problem and if forced will result in significant chip outs. In these cases reverse the direction of the cut, but now be careful on the other side.

As the trough deepens, use progressively wider #9's to widen the channel. Use scrapers to remove carving tool facets and to blend surfaces. The goal is to get a continuously, uniform, undulating surface between the high spots and the low. Ideally each lobe will taper as it approaches the medallion and each trough will appear to taper in a similar way. Figure 10-32 shows intermediate progress and figure 10-33 shows the completed process. Repeat these steps on the remaining lobes.

A few fine points to strive for are a continuous surface that feathers smoothly into the ridge line at the perimeter. This will give a clean line around the perimeter that looks better than one that is thicker and not sinuous. This is best achieved with scrapers. Straight, radial lobes

10-35 The completed concave shell.

10-36 A completed and finished concave shell from the kneehole bureau.

that are well defined. The depth of the overall sculpting of the shell interior will determine how quickly the wide part of a lobe at the perimeter will dive down as it goes towards that medallion. The steeper the drop, the more dramatic the look.

The medallion for this concave shell is identical to the one already presented in the Convex Newport

Shell chapter. Thus, it will not be discussed again here. Refer to the convex shell discussion. Figure 10-34 shows the medallion complete and figure 10-35 shows the completed concave shell. Figure 10-36 shows a completed and finished concave shell that is the door for a Newport kneehole bureau.

About the Author

Tony Kubalak builds Queen Anne and Chippendale reproductions in his basement workshop in Eagan, MN. His main interest is to faithfully reproduce the finest pieces of 18th century American Furniture. He has studied with Gene Landon at the Olde Mill Cabinet Shoppe for several years. His work has been featured in *Fine Woodworking Magazine, Woodwork Magazine, Woodshop News, Eagan Magazine* and *Midwest Home Magazine.* In addition he has written articles for *Fine Woodworking, Woodwork and American Period Furniture,* the annual journal of the Society of American Period Furniture Makers. Furthermore, his work has won several awards including Best Carving, Best Handwork and Best Traditional Design at the Northern Woods Exhibition, which is an annual display and competition sponsored by the Minnesota Woodworkers Guild. He has also been recognized nationally every year since 2005 by being selected for the Directory of Traditional American Crafts®, which is sponsored by *Early American Life Magazine.* You can see more of his work by visiting his website at: www.TonyKubalak.com.

Imperial to Metric Conversion

Inches	mm*	inches	mm*	inches	mm
1/64	0.40	33/64	13.10	1	25.4
1/32	0.79	17/32	13.49	2	50.8
3/64	1.19	35/64	13.89	3	76.2
1/16	1.59	9/16	14.29	4	101.6
5/64	1.98	37/64	14.68	5	127.0
3/32	2.38	19/32	15.08	6	152.4
7/64	2.78	39/64	15.48	7	177.8
1/8	3.18	5/8	15.88	8	203.2
9/64	3.57	41/64	16.27	9	228.6
5/32	3.97	21/32	16.67	10	254.0
11/64	4.37	43/64	17.07	11	279.4
3/16	4.76	11/16	17.46	12	304.8
13/64	5.16	45/64	17.86	13	330.2
7/32	5.56	23/32	18.26	14	355.6
15/64	5.95	47/64	18.65	15	381.0
1/4	6.35	3/4	19.05	16	406.4
17/64	6.75	49/64	19.45	17	431.8
9/32	7.14	25/32	19.84	18	457.2
19/64	7.54	51/64	20.24	19	482.6
5/16	7.94	13/16	20.64	20	508.0
21/64	8.33	53/64	21.03	21	533.4
11/32	8.73	27/32	21.43	22	558.8
23/64	9.13	55/64	21.83	23	584.2
3/8	9.53	7/8	22.23	24	609.6
25/64	9.92	57/64	22.62	25	635.0
13/32	10.32	29/32	23.02	26	660.4
27/64	10.72	59/64	23.42	27	685.8
7/16	11.11	15/16	23.81	28	711.2
29/64	11.51	61/64	24.21	29	736.6
15/32	11.91	31/32	24.61	30	762.0
31/64	12.30	63/64	25.00	31	787.4
1/2	12.70	1 inch	25.40	32	812.8

*Rounded to the nearest 0.01 mm